THE PLAGUE MAKERS

Wendy Barnaby is a science writer and broadcaster. After graduating from Sydney University, she began her career in the Australian diplomatic service. She has since worked as a journalist in Sweden and Great Britain, where she broadcasts regularly for the BBC and the Australian Broadcasting Company. From 1992 to 1995, she chaired the Association of British Science Writers. She is married to defense analyst Dr Frank Barnaby and they have two grown-up children.

THE PLAGUE MAKERS

The Secret World of Biological Warfare

New Revised Edition

Wendy Barnaby

CONTINUUM
NEW YORK

2000

The Continuum International Publishing Group Inc
370 Lexington Avenue, New York, NY 10017

Collection and introduction Copyright © 1999 by Wendy Barnaby
Cover art © 1999 by Nikolai Globe

Original edition published in Great Britain in 1999 by Vision Paperbacks,
20 Queen Anne Street, London W1M 0AY UK
a division of Satin Publications Ltd

Printed in the United States of America

Library of Congress Cataloging-in-Publication Data

Barnaby, Wendy
    The plague makers : the secret world of biological warfare / Wendy
Barnaby—New rev. ed.
        p. cm.
    Includes bibliographical references and index.
    ISBN 0-8264-1258-0 (alk. paper)
    1. Biological warfare.   2. World politics—1989–   I. Title.
UG447.8.B34 2000
358'.38—dc21

                                        00-038337

For Frank, Sophie and Ben

ACKNOWLEDGMENTS

I would like to thank Geof Allenby, Ian Doucet, Dr John Field, Professor Erhard Geissler, Sue Holmes, Dr Neil Keyworth, Andrew Rutter, Nicholas Sims, Dr Peter Turnbull, John Walker, Simon Whitby, Richard Whittaker and Henrietta Wilson for their help during the preparation of this book.

I am particularly grateful to the following people, who read and commented on parts of the manuscript: Professor Malcolm Dando, Dr Graham Lloyd, Dr Graham Pearson, Julian Perry Robinson and Professor Harry Smith. They are not responsible for the opinions expressed; and if, in spite of their best efforts, there are still factual errors, the fault is mine.

CONTENTS

INTRODUCTION

New York, summer 1999. Dozens of crows around the Bronx Zoo lost their balance, became unable to fly and died. Dr Tracey McNamara, head of the Zoo's pathology department, sat there saying, "It's raining crows." Over the Labor Day weekend, birds in the Zoo itself sickened, then died: a cormorant, three Chilean flamingoes, a pheasant and a bald eagle. At about the same time, two elderly people in Queens died of a strange encephalitis caused by a virus their doctor was unable to diagnose. She sent it to the New York City Department of Health, who forwarded it to a laboratory of the federal Centers for Disease Control and Prevention (CDC) in Fort Collins, Colorado. The CDC announced on 3 September that it was St Louis encephalitis, a virus spread around by mosquitoes. New York's Mayor Giuliani drew up plans to spray New York with malathion to kill them.

Meanwhile Dr McNamara was analysing bird samples and becoming suspicious. St Louis encephalitis does not normally kill birds. Could a new virus be killing both the birds and the people? Dr McNamara sent samples to the CDC and the National Veterinary Services Laboratory in Ames, Iowa. Ames's analysis convinced her that the virus was something new and she tried to alert the CDC, but nobody there returned her calls. Unwilling to wait, she sent samples to the US Army Medical Research Institute of Infectious Diseases (USAMRIID), whose scientists are experts in biological warfare and bioterrorism. On 22 September USAMRIID confirmed that the virus was not St Louis. The CDC was by now putting the puzzle together, and on 24 September made a public announcement that the virus was in fact a form of West Nile virus—a disease never before found in the United States. From a public health perspective the re-diagnosis was unimportant: West Nile virus is carried by birds and spread by mosquitoes, and malathion would have been used for spraying them anyway.

But the change in diagnosis rang mental bells in Langley, Virginia, where the CIA's bioweapons analysis section is familiar with viruses that could be used to attack populations. The West Nile virus had been described in a book published in the UK earlier in the year, as being one which Iraqi President Saddam Hussein was planning to use in a bioterrorist attack.

Bioterrorism inflicts damage on a people or an economy. Deliberately introducing a virus would be one way of causing death and disruption. To do that would be to wage biological war. It has been dubbed "public health in reverse."

Biological war uses living micro-organisms—bacteria, viruses and so on—to cause disease or death in people, animals and plants. It is not like a bullet which kills as a result of its initial impact. It depends for its destruction on the organisms' ability to live and multiply in the targeted person, animal or plant, causing infection to take hold and illness to debilitate or kill. Death is not instantaneous: it follows the symptoms and progression of whatever disease has been introduced. As well as disease agents like bacteria which are themselves alive, biological warfare agents are generally held to include poisons which are made by living things: toxins from plants or animals.

Of all hostilities, there is something particularly repugnant about biological warfare. Nevertheless, many nations have developed biological weapons. Many experts fear that biological warfare is becoming more of a threat. At the end of 1996, the United States government said it believed that, in the last twenty years, the number of countries which either have or are trying to develop biological weapons has doubled.

This book examines why this is so.

At least 50 people in New York came down with West Nile virus, and at least five died. Meanwhile, crows began dying in New Jersey: south of New York City. South was the direction the birds were migrating. Officials were not sure whether the virus would survive the winter in New York. It may break out again there in future summers. It may be carried to South America, with the birds.

Experts disagree about the likelihood of the New York outbreak being a biological warfare attack. Dr Ken Alibek, deputy chief of research for the Soviet Union's biowarfare program until he defected to the US in 1992, thought it was suspicious. "It will not be possible to say whether or not it is terrorism unless we have a thorough study," he told people on Capitol Hill. Jessica Stern, at Harvard's Center for Science and International Affairs, rated the probability as "highly unlikely." "For one thing, West Nile encephalitis is a relatively mild disease, and Saddam Hussein has far more virulent agents in his arsenal," she wrote. It seems more likely that the virus arrived in the US in the same way that most others do—in carrier people and animals, and undetected until they cause illness.

Trying to monitor passengers arriving in the US for viruses is well nigh impossible, not least because any illness may not show up until days after a person has entered the country. The only hope is for officials to liase with hospitals. Agricultural pests and diseases are similarly brought into the US in sausages and other, more exotic, imports. Recently, Federal Agriculture Department officials reported that someone brought two bucketloads of live Vietnamese snails into Los Angeles International Airport. The snails are voracious rice pests. Had they escaped, they could have caused tremendous damage. In the early 1970s, Newcastle disease attacked poultry and other birds in southern California. Nearly 12 million chickens and other birds had to be killed. The eradication effort and the losses amounted to $56 million. Agriculture officials said that the virus was probably carried in to the US by parrots imported from South America. Most imported bugs come unintentionally. But some are brought in or made to cause disease deliberately. In the last few years, both official and public awareness of the biological warfare threat has grown.

"The most serious threat to our security may consist of unannounced attacks on American cities by sub-national groups using genetically-engineered pathogens," concluded the Pentagon-funded US Commission on National Security in the 21st Century. "States, terrorists and other disaffected groups will acquire weapons of mass destruction . . . and some of them will use them," it reports. Local preparedness for terrorist attacks has been stepped

up in the US. During fiscal year 2000, it will cost the Clinton administration $1.4 billion—nearly double last year's budget. Fire-
fighters, police officers and emergency medical personnel—"first
responders"—are undergoing training in 120 cities across the country. This has resulted from the Nunn-Lugar-Domenici amendment
to the 1997 Defense Authorization Act, which called for better
training, equipment and coordination amongst personnel who
would be in the front line of dealing with terrorism. The Pentagon-
led initiative, which involves many other federal agencies, is training first responders in how to approach the scene of an attack, how
to identify toxic agents, and how to handle detectors, protective
clothing and decontamination equipment. Another Pentagon initiative plans to develop National Guard Rapid Assessment and Initial Detection (RAID) teams to act alongside the first responders.
The year 2000 will see the first ten of a planned 54 RAID teams deployed. Some germ warfare experts are skeptical of their value.
Said Amy Smithson of the Henry L. Stimson Center in Washington:
"There is no way that these teams, even if deployed in six hours,
would be there in time to make any difference. This is a very poor
answer and a waste of taxpayers' money."

Public awareness of the bioterrorist threat has also grown in recent years. In February 1998, the FBI arrested Larry Wayne Harris.
A microbiologist belonging to a white supremicist group called
Aryan Nations, Harris had already been charged in 1995 as a result
of ordering vials of plague bacteria through the mail. This time he
boasted that he possessed military-grade anthrax—enough to
"wipe out" Las Vegas. His arsenal proved an empty threat: a harmless veterinary vaccine against anthrax. The second scare, reported
the next month, was that the UK was supposedly at risk from anthrax allegedly smuggled in by Saddam Hussein. No anthrax was
found, but the international dimensions of bioterrorism were put
in the spotlight in the UK press. In April, FBI Director Louis J. Freeh
testified before a congressional hearing that the number of possible
terrorist incidents reported to the FBI had increased dramatically.
The US press took up the story, even though 80 per cent of the reports were hoaxes. In May, President Clinton chose a US Naval
Academy Commencement to announce that a national stockpile of

vaccines and antibiotics would be distributed across the country, to be used in any bioterrorist incident.

There are several current concerns about bioterrorism. The threat is not so much that dissident groups might cause thousands of deaths through unleashing microorganisms in public places. Attacks on a large scale need technical abilities which very small groups are unlikely to muster. They could still, however, carry out localised releases—especially in food—which would sicken and kill relatively small numbers of people but cause widespread panic and economic disruption. The other fear about bioterrorism is that a small group might be helped by a government to stage an attack. If a rogue power wanted to lash out at the United States, then it might be tempted to use chemical or biological weapons either directly or by arming a terrorist group. And now that the Russian economy has collapsed, there are scientists who worked on the biological weapons program there who might well be tempted by a lucrative offer to provide their knowledge to terrorists. In an effort to prevent this, the US has funded programs to finance some of these scientists in legitimate research on vaccines and anti-viral drugs.

Certainly, worries about the number of states able and willing to make their own biological weapons have grown. Some estimates suggest there may be ten such states at the moment: Russia, Iraq, China, India, Iran, Israel, North Korea, Libya, Taiwan and Syria. Under the apartheid regime, South Africa also developed biological-weapon devices for sabotage and murder. For many countries, the main lesson of the Gulf War was that they could not afford to confront the West without recourse to weapons of mass destruction. Biological weapons are the most easily obtained of these. Unable to compete with the technologically superior and nuclear-armed Western Alliance, some states may turn to biological weapons—the poor man's nuclear bomb—as a counter.

1999 saw the final collapse of the United Nations Special Commission on Iraq, set up after the Gulf War to supervise the destruction of Iraq's chemical and biological weapons and their means of delivery. Its disintegration began in the autumn of 1997, when Iraqi officials insisted that some areas of their country should be off-limits to the UNSCOM inspectors. In October, Baghdad expelled all seven US members of an UNSCOM inspection team and branded them as spies working under false pretexts. The crisis lurched from one confrontation to another, involving at various times diplomatic intervention by the Russians and by the UN Secretary-General Kofi Annan, who succeeded in drawing up a Memorandum of Understanding (MOU) between the UN and the Republic of Iraq. Signed in Baghdad on 23 February 1998, it appeared to allow UNSCOM to continue its work; but by late summer 1998, the MOU had unravelled. Relations continued to deteriorate through the autumn, with Iraq demanding an immediate end to sanctions, and on 28 September, Iraq made clear that it had no intention of resuming full cooperation with UNSCOM inspectors in the near future. Iraqi Deputy Prime Minister Tariq Aziz and UN Secretary-General Kofi Annan met to discuss proposals for resuming the sanctions reviews; however, Aziz dismissed the inspections as "provocations." On 11 December, President Clinton and UK Prime Minister Tony Blair launched four days of air attacks on Iraq to punish Baghdad for its obstruction.

The situation remained unresolved during 1999. The five permanent members of the UN Security Council—the United States, Russia, Britain, China and France—found it hard to agree how to go forward, with the US ranged against Russia and China in their agreement on the immediate lifting of sanctions, with Britain and France in the middle. Against the opposition of the other three, the US and Britain continued their air attacks on Iraqi targets in the northern and southern "no-fly" zones of the country. In December 1999, Iraq rejected a UN proposal, endorsed by a Security Council resolution, that sanctions would be lifted for a trial period of 120 days in return for renewed cooperation with UN weapons inspectors. Declared Khalid al-Douri, head of the Iraqi parliament's Arab and Foreign Relations Committee, "Iraq does not accept the new resolution and will not accept any decision which does not lift the embargo without any restrictions or conditions." By this time, many observers were predicting that the sanctions would be lifted during 2000 in any case, and hundreds of Western firms were courting the Iraqi regime in the hope of winning contracts for reconstructing the country when sanctions are lifted.

There will be a mass of reconstruction to do. The sanctions appear not to have touched the leaders of the regime, but they have denied the civilian population adequate food, clean water and medical facilities. Inevitably, the old and the young have been particularly affected. In August 1999, the UN Children's Fund (UNICEF) reported the results of a major survey into child death rates in Iraq. It found that children under five years old in central and southern parts of the country "are dying at more than twice the rate they were ten years ago." UNICEF continued: "Even if not all suffering in Iraq can be imputed to external factors, especially sanctions, the Iraqi people would not be undergoing such deprivations in the absence of the prolonged measures imposed by the Security Council and the effects of war." Said Dennis Halliday, former UN Humanitarian Coordinator for Iraq: "We are in the process of destroying an entire society. It is as simple and terrifying as that."

Iraqi President Saddam Hussein is widely assumed to harbor significant stocks of biological (and chemical) weapons. The whole sorry saga illustrates the futility of the international community trying to stop a nation determined to develop its own biological weapons, in the absence of the political will to do so.

At the beginning of the 21st century, there are both frightening and encouraging developments in biological weapons.

The scary scenario is not just that bioterrorism will increase. It is that biological weapons will be targeted at specific groups of people, according to their genetic make-up. As early as 1997, researchers published a paper in the *American Journal of Human Genetics* asserting that they could distinguish between African Americans, European Americans and Hispanic Americans on the basis of the differences in the groups' genes. With rapid advances in genetics, experts expect that genetic weapons will be able to distinguish between groups with as few as hundreds of thousands of members within the next ten years. This would bring a new and horrifying sophistication to ethnic cleansing.

All, however, is not doom and gloom. One bright spot on the horizon is the progress being made by the international community to conclude a verification protocol for the Biological Weapons Convention (BWC).

Negotiated in 1972, the BWC outlaws biological weapons as a class—the first arms control agreement to do so. Along with their undertakings not to "develop, produce, stockpile or otherwise acquire or attain" any sort of biological weapons, however, the signatories were not required to take on any obligations to make sure they were honouring this commitment. And, as Russia, Iraq and South Africa have since proved, ratification of the Convention has not been a bar to the development of biological weapons, whether on a large or small scale.

For several years now, the international community has been trying to negotiate a so-called verification protocol, which would enable states to promote compliance to the BWC.

The negotiations have been long and difficult. The pharmaceutical industry in the US has been reluctant to accept on-site visits, designed to confirm the declarations they would be required to make about their research. The industry has feared the visits could provide a cover for industrial espionage. Recently, however, significant progress has been made on this front, with wide acceptance of a package of non-confrontational visits that could be made to ensure that a country's declarations were accurate and complete. Such visits would be completely separate from investigations that would be carried out if any country's activities fell under suspicion.

It is hoped that a verification protocol will be finalised and adopted by a special conference of States Parties in 2000. The achievement would be a fitting 75th anniversary of the 1925 Geneva Protocol, the first international attempt specifically to prohibit the use of "bacteriological methods of warfare."

Whatever the safeguards against biological warfare, it has become obvious that the world will only escape its ravages if the international community has enough political will to prevent it. Countries need to take and sustain measures designed to contain the threat, and to emphasise the moral repugnance of using such weapons.

The first chapter of this book sets out why concern about the threat of biological weapons is growing. Chapter 2 looks more closely at the nature of biological weapons, the agents they might contain and what effects they would have. The next two chapters look at elements of the threat: terrorism and Iraq's secret biological weapons. Their clandestine efforts to develop such weapons are by no means the first. Since the 1920s, the Western allies, Japan, the former Soviet Union and South Africa have all done extensive work on agents and weapons. Chapters 5 and 6 review these programmes, describing how weapons were both prepared for use and actually used. Chapter 7 returns to another element of the growing threat: current scientific developments that make the spread of biological agents more likely and raise the possibility of horrifying new types of weapons. Chapter 8 explores what defence is possible against biological attack and what problems it involves. The next chapter surveys international efforts to prevent the spread of biological weapons, and the final one asks what the role of scientists and citizens might be in bolstering these attempts to make the world a safer place.

WENDY BARNABY
Stockbridge
January 2000

1

THE GROWING THREAT

. . . And *here's some news just in. Sources in Hong Kong say a lethal epidemic is raging in the Prince of Wales Barracks, the British Army base on the island. Thirty-two personnel have died in the past 24 hours, and over a hundred more are gravely ill. The sources say that all the affected troops were at a dinner on Wednesday evening in honour of the visiting Defence Secretary, who is himself among the casualties. The Ministry of Defence has refused to comment on the reports. Tension has been rising on the island as Britain prepares to hand power over to the Chinese. Many local people have accused the British authorities of failing to secure their civil and political rights under the Chinese regime.*

This fictitious news flash could well be broadcast after a biological warfare (BW) attack. The weapon?—10 milligrams of botulinal toxin, emptied into a bulk container of pasteurised milk in a processing plant whose dairy products supplied the military base. Each portion of ice cream made from the milk would be liberally laced with the toxin: 10 milligrams, after all, is enough to kill 25,000 people. The guests at the banquet would be seized with nausea, vomiting, cramps, double vision and muscular paralysis. Up to half of them would probably die. A determined worker with access to the processing plant could easily slip the toxin in. Ten milligrams is just one-fiftieth of the weight of a paper clip.

Biological weapons have long been contentious. As early as 1899 and 1907, The Hague Conventions condemned and prohibited the use of poison and pathogens in war. Most people instinctively recoil from such weapons, and an idea has grown that they are not effective military weapons. This chapter argues that, certainly since the Second World War they have been known to be weapons of mass destruction, but that a myth has grown up suggesting they are not useful. Current developments demonstrate just how dangerous these weapons are, and underline the need for them to be controlled. While governments are in the best position to do this, citizens have a role to play as well; and the last chapter discusses what contribution they can make.

Any discussion of BW, however, should start by acknowledging that it is a form of warfare probably as old as war itself.

AN ANCIENT IDEA

BW attacks have a very long history. Early Persians, Greeks and Romans poisoned their enemies' wells by throwing corpses into them. The three-year siege of Caffa (now Feodosija) was broken in 1346 when attacking Tartars slung the bodies of plague victims over the walls and infected the inhabitants. An eyewitness reported: "The Tartars, fatigued by such a plague and pestiferous disease, stupefied and amazed, observing themselves dying without hope of health, ordered cadavers placed on their hurling machines and thrown into the city of Caffa, so that by means of these intolerable passengers the defenders died widely. Thus there were projected mountains of dead, nor could the Christians hide or flee, or be freed from such disaster."[1] The same tactic is said to have been used in 1710 by Russian besiegers trying to dislodge Swedish soldiers from their city of Reval. Both the French and the British used BW in North America in the eighteenth century. In 1763, in an attempt to kill North American Indians, a British Captain presented two Indian chiefs with a lethal gift. He reported: "Out of our regard for them, we gave them two blankets and a handkerchief out of the small-pox hospital. I hope it will have the desired effect."[2] The disease took hold among the local Indian tribes.

Today, we do not need to resort to such crude methods to infect people, their animals and crops with disease. Modern biologists know what organisms cause different illnesses, and they can grow bacteria and other causative agents. Delivered in ways specially designed to preserve and spread them, the agents are usually breathed in by people or animals or added to their food or water. They may be directly injected in needles or by insects, or sprayed onto plants or the soil they grow in. No matter what the method of delivery, however, this form of attack is generally regarded as barbaric.

BW: BARBARIC WARFARE

BW has long been regarded as especially odious. Ancient Brahmin law demanded of a warrior that "Fighting in a battle, he should not kill his enemies with weapons that are concealed, barbed or smeared with poison."[3] The Roman jurists declared *armis bella non venenis geri*—"War is waged with weapons, not with poison."

The 1925 Geneva Protocol was the culmination of the first international attempts to address biological warfare. Uppermost in the minds of the nations who negotiated it was their experience of chemical weapons in the trenches of the First World War, which the Protocol declares to be "justly condemned by the general opinion of the civilised world." It prohibits the use of chemical weapons, and extends that prohibition to "bacteriological methods of warfare." The most recent international convention to deal with biological weapons says that their use "would be repugnant to the conscience of mankind." We will return to this agreement (the Biological Weapons Convention of 1972) in Chapter 9.

These international treaties reflect our intuitive disgust for biological warfare. We recoil at the idea of killing by infection and disease. Something like bacteria, which are invisible to the naked eye, seem especially threatening. It is also horrifying that our need to breathe makes us vulnerable to whatever is in the air we take in. Soldiers who suspect they may be exposed to BW attacks wear special masks which protect them, but most countries do not supply these to civilians. The most vulnerable of them will be the young, old and infirm.

The fear provoked by biological attack also make these weapons peculiarly horrible. When large numbers of people suddenly and inexplicably become ill and die, the very social and moral basis of society is threatened. Between 1346 and 1350, the Black Death killed one-third of Europe's population, including the inhabitants of two hundred thousand towns and villages. The psychological impact of the complete collapse of everything people had taken for granted was profound. Chronicles of the time reveal a heart-rending picture of chaos and despair (see box, page 28).

Developing biological weapons means understanding what diseases are, how they are caused and treated, and how we can protect ourselves against them. For this we look to medical science. The idea that medicine should be turned on its head and used to infect and kill is outrageous. It is completely contrary to medical ethics, enshrined for 2000 years in the Hippocratic Oath which directs doctors to work for the benefit of the sick and not the reverse. Our shock and abhorrence for medical research thus distorted is summed up in a story told by the veteran science journalist Lord Ritchie Calder. He once asked a scientist involved in "defence biology" what he was working for. The answer was "a cure for metabolism."[4]

Moral reasons are, however, not the only grounds for opposition to biological weapons. Scepticism about their effectiveness has grown up as well.

BELIEVABLE WEAPONS?

The main reason for doubt about the utility of biological weapons is that they have been labelled too unpredictable and uncontrollable. This is because of the way they are delivered (which we will look at more closely in Chapter 4). In order to be breathed in or ingested, they need to be released into the environment, and are therefore at the mercy of wind and sunshine which can kill them or blow them off target. This means they may only be effective in a limited range of circumstances. Although received wisdom is still that biological weapons are militarily unimportant, this judgement is increasingly being questioned. It is now argued that doubts about the weapons' usefulness may simply have been a rationalisation for the fact that President Nixon renounced the US's considerable offensive biological weapons capability in 1969, confining the country to defence only. If the weapons were not to be produced, the argument runs, they had to be proclaimed as being not worth producing.

A very different interpretation of Nixon's decision has been offered by Professor Matthew Meselson of Harvard University, who has long campaigned to limit the spread and use of biological weapons. He has argued that the US programme had shown just how dangerous and easily produced biological weapons were; and that there would be no way of stopping other countries producing them. The US realised its own programme was a threat to its own security.[5] Thus what appeared to be either an admission that biological weapons were useless, or an altruistic gesture for the benefit of world peace, was actually a hard-headed calculation of the best course of action to safeguard US security.

This analysis is supported by Gradon Carter, of Britain's Protection and Life Sciences Division of the Defence Evaluation Research Agency (the establishment which does biological defence work) at Porton Down.[6] Nixon, he argues, wanted "to draw attention away from the longer established and proven chemical capability recently used in Vietnam, [and] to placate congressional, national and international concern ... Domestic political considerations were the main motivation ..."[7] He points out that by 1969, "The utility of BW had been demonstrated by all means short of use in war ... the US had sustained its offensive BW capability for nearly a quarter of a century. During this period, the concept of uncontrollability and unpredictability ... had not arisen."[8] There can be no doubt that some Americans knew exactly what biological weapons were capable of, and how they could be used.

Other countries have been similarly impressed. They have developed their own biological weapons programmes.

WHO HAS BIOLOGICAL WEAPONS?

The two countries which are known to have biological weapons are Iraq and Russia; and it has largely been the discovery of their clandestine programmes which has rung BW alarm bells in the 1990's. The Russians admitted in 1992 that they had been developing biological weapons in spite of their undertaking (under the Biological Weapons Convention) not to; and in 1995 Iraq's extensive BW programme was finally uncovered, following the Gulf War. We will look at both of these events in more detail later on (Chapters 3 and 6). South Africa has also developed BW devices for political assassination.

Other countries are suspected of developing biological weapons. One UK estimate from Jane's Consultancy Services[9] puts the number at 16 who certainly, probably or possibly have them, with a further four as doubtful. The two which are known to have BW are Iraq and Russia. The fourteen whose status is unclear to the Jane's author are Belarus, People's Republic of China, Egypt, India, Iran, Israel, North Korea, South Korea, Libya, Pakistan, South Africa, Syria, Taiwan and the Ukraine. The four doubtfuls are Algeria, Cuba, Jordan and Kazakhstan. Another survey, by the Office of Technology Assessment of the US Congress in 1993, identified Iran, Iraq, Israel, Libya, Syria, China, North Korea and Taiwan as "generally reported as having undeclared offensive biological warfare programmes."[10]

The list is instructive: it comprises nations neither rich nor poor, which have a cadre of scientists but which are not at the forefront of scientific research. Such nations (over 100 in 1988) have the technological capacity to make BW which are, compared with nuclear weapons, cheap, quick and easy to manufacture. The US Congress Office of Technology Assessment estimates that ten million US dollars would allow a country to develop a large arsenal. A similar arsenal of nuclear weapons would cost $200 million; of chemical weapons, tens of millions.[11] Evidence presented to a United Nations panel in 1969 estimated that "for a large-scale operation against a civilian population, casualties might cost about $2000 per square kilometre with conventional weapons, $800 with nuclear weapons, $600 with nerve-gas weapons and just $1 with biological weapons."[12]

The US government considers that the attractions of biological weapons are increasing. In November 1996, the leader of the US delegation to the Fourth Review Conference of the Biological Weapons Convention said that the US believes that twice as many states are now seeking a BW capability as when the Convention came into force, in 1975.

WHY HAVE BIOLOGICAL WEAPONS?

Biological weapons have been called "a poor man's nuclear weapon." They are a cheap way of acquiring a weapon of mass destruction with the psychological effect that entails. The possibility of an attack generates fear amongst populations, which in itself puts pressure on political and military leaders and alters strategic thinking.

Biological weapons could be unleashed on a mass scale in a revenge attack against civilian populations. They could also be used to flex national muscles, to disrupt an enemy's preparations for war or to weaken or kill enemy troops. Vulnerable targets for BW attack include concentrations of soldiers in fortified areas, naval task forces, assembly areas and military bases. BW aimed at crops could be used to weaken the economy of another country, possibly before an attack with conventional weapons. BW might also be used against dissident minorities within a state, in the way Saddam Hussein used chemical weapons against his Kurdish population at Halabja in 1988. Rulers who would be prepared to use them in this way would probably not be deterred by the possibility of others being killed at the same time.

If a country were at war, biological attacks would overload already-stretched medical facilities. In Moscow, in January 1960, one person with smallpox infected forty-six others, three of whom died. The authorities immediately mobilized 5,500 vaccination teams which vaccinated 6,372,376 people within a week. They also followed up everyone who had been in contact with anyone who developed the disease. This meant searching a large area of the country. They found 9,000 whom they put under medical supervision—662 of whom had to be hospitalised.[13] A similar incident happened in the US in 1947, when a businessman took a bus from Mexico City to New York City. He became ill during the journey but went sightseeing in New York for several hours, walking around the city and through a major department store. Nine days later he died—also of smallpox. He had infected 12 other people, two of whom also died, and as a result of this outbreak public health officials arranged for 6,350,000 people in New York city alone to be vaccinated within a few weeks.[14]

Disguised attacks

When there are no open hostilities, biological weapons could be used under the guise of natural outbreaks of disease. This would make it impossible to blame the perpetrator. There have been incidents of suspected but unprovable attacks. In the 1970s, for example, Cuba accused the US of being responsible for outbreaks of blue mould on its tobacco crops, cane smut on its sugar cane, African swine fever in its livestock and even haemorrhagic dengue fever amongst its people. These blights were not unknown in Cuba and it was impossible to tell whether these particular outbreaks had occurred naturally or as the result of deliberate action.

These then are the reasons why biological weapons should not be dismissed as worthless, impractical or unusable. Added to these, however, are some recent worrying events which make their development seem much more likely.

WHY WORRY?

Terrorism

One of the shields against biological attack has been our inability to imagine the use of indiscriminate weapons against civilians. This psychological threshold was crossed in March, 1995, when the Japanese sect called Aum Shinrikyo unleashed chemical weapons against commuters in the Tokyo subway. Once the unthinkable has been done, it becomes more thinkable. Chapter 3 examines the terrorist threat in more detail. It is enough to underline here that it is causing increasing concern.

Even as the terrorist threat is growing, scientific developments are making it far easier than before to produce biological weapons secretly.

Widespread technology

The biotechnology industry which is now thriving in countries with any reasonable scientific infrastructure provides the equipment needed for making biological agents. No special tools are needed. We look into this in more detail in Chapter 5; however we should note now that the technology needed for making agents for weapons is the same as that used for completely innocent agricultural and medical ends: the production of feed for livestock, as well as vaccines and antibiotics. This means that weapons plants can masquerade as civilian installations. The deception is of course desirable from the producer's point of view, but the fact that it is so easily done underlines the routine nature of the equipment needed. The knowledge is also easily available in the open scientific literature.

Fears that legitimate science might disguise illegal BW programmes were proved to be justified when, in 1995, the full extent of Iraq's arsenal became known. Even though they were not used in the Gulf War, the fact that its biological agents were weaponized and deployed for use sent shudders down many spines.

There are fears, too, about the exodus of scientists from the Soviet Union following the chaos of its break-up in 1991. It is estimated that five per cent of all Russia's scientists have emigrated since then, escaping political instability and economic hardship because of unpaid salaries. Most have gone to the United States; some to Israel; some, it is assumed, to other countries where their expertise will have come as a welcome boost to fledgling biological warfare programmes.

Even as the technological means and know-how are spreading, there is another scientific development which could make BW a far more flexible option. And that is genetic engineering.

Genetic engineering

Now that researchers are beginning to understand the genetic structures of organisms, they are learning how to change them to make different organisms with new properties—ones that could make them into more effective agents for weapons. It may turn them from slow-acting, unstable organisms, or ones which persist in the environment, into fast-acting, more reliable ones which might die after a specified time or in certain environmental conditions. This would increase their specificity. In addition, it may be possible to make biological weapons which would only attack certain ethnic groups. We will examine these horrifying possibilities in more detail in Chapter 7. They do point, along with the other developments above, to the increasing threat that biological weapons pose.

After decades of obscurity, biological weapons have a new urgency on the international security agenda. The discovery of secret BW programmes in Iraq, South Africa and the former Soviet Union, the upsurge of terrorism and the spread of biotechnology, along with the longer-term threat of genetic engineering, have all revived interest in them in the 1990's. Far from being militarily useless, they are recognised to pose a lethal threat in specific situations. The next chapter takes a closer look at what biological weapons might contain, and what their effects might be.

PLAGUE

The plague which struck Sicily in 1347 was a fearsome illness. Michael of Piazza, a Franciscan friar, described it like this: "Those infected felt themselves penetrated by a pain throughout their whole bodies and, so to say, undermined. Then there developed on the thighs or upper arms a boil about the size of a lentil which the people called 'burn boil'. This infected the whole body, and penetrated it so that the patient violently vomited blood. This vomiting of blood continued without intermission for three days, there being no means of healing it, and then the patient expired . . . The town of Catania lost all its inhabitants, and ultimately sank into complete oblivion. Here not only the 'burn blisters' appeared, but there developed gland boils on the sexual organs, the thighs, the arms, or on the neck. At first these were of the size of a hazel nut, and developed accompanied by violent fits . . . Soon the boils grew to the size of a walnut, then to that of a hen's egg or a goose's egg, and they were exceedingly painful, and irritated the body, causing the sufferer to vomit blood. The blood rose from the affected lungs to the throat, producing on the whole body a putrefying and ultimately decomposing effect . . ."[15]

Such a ghastly, highly contagious disease—"anyone who only spoke to them was seized . . . and in no manner could evade death"—caused not only panic but the complete breakdown of social bonds and relationships: "Then there was no love, no faithfulness, no trust. No neighbour would lend a helping hand to another . . . The patient lay helpless and forsaken in his dwelling, no relation came near him, at the most his best friends were huddled up in some corner. The physician did not dare to visit him, the terrified priest trembling offered the Sacraments of the Church. With heart-rending supplication children called for their parents, parents for their children, the husband for the help of his wife: 'I am a thirst, give me at least one drop of water. I am still alive. Do not be afraid of me!' "[16]

ASSASSINATION

On 7 September 1978, Georgi Markov was walking from Waterloo Bridge to the Strand offices of the BBC, when he felt a sharp pain in his thigh. He turned round to find a man picking up an umbrella and apologising. Next day he was rushed to hospital with a fever and falling blood pressure. Four days after the attack he died. At the point at which the umbrella had pierced his thigh, doctors found, embedded in his flesh, a tiny metal pellet with four holes in it. The pellet was found to have contained ricin, a highly toxic poison made from the seeds of the castor oil plant.

Markov was a writer who had defected from Bulgaria, and who had dared to make broadcasts on the BBC and Radio Free Europe criticising the regime of the then Bulgarian President Todor Zhivkov. It was the Bulgarian secret police who had assassinated him. They had used the same method, ten days earlier, in an attempt to kill another Bulgarian journalist in exile in Paris; but he had survived because they had not used enough ricin in the pellet.

A few days after Markov's death, his wife Annabel was interviewed on the BBC. She said: "All I know is that my husband was a strong man; a healthy man. The doctors said he had the constitution of an ox. He came home on Thursday night—he was perfectly OK—and by the next day he was in a critical situation. He told me the most extraordinary story, that he'd been jabbed with an umbrella tip. It was almost as if he didn't want to believe it himself, and I don't think he wanted to frighten me with it. But he showed me the mark the umbrella had made—like the point of a hypodermic. He'd made it clear in the past that if he was killed he'd know what organisation was behind it. He was conscious right up to the end and I was with him until he died. He talked about us. He didn't talk to me about being poisoned but he did to other people and I think it was because he didn't want to distress me or alarm me.

Before he defected he was one of the top writers in Bulgaria. He was in a very privileged little circle. He knew things about people in Bulgaria which very few other people knew. He was trying to expose corruption."

Former KGB General Oleg Kalugin has admitted that the assassination was carried out on Zhivkov's orders, but nobody has ever been convicted for the murder. Scotland Yard regards the case as still open, and the British government is currently pursuing it with Bulgarian President Petar Stoyanov.

2

AGENTS OF BIOLOGICAL WARFARE

"**A**nthrax, sprayed from the back of an aircraft on a cool, calm night, could take out all of Washington DC. This could cause up to 3 million fatalities compared to 2 million from a hydrogen bomb."[1] This is how Dr Graham Pearson, former Director of the UK's biological defence establishment at Porton Down, rates the destructive potential of biological versus nuclear weapons.

This chapter takes a closer look at the agents of biological warfare, and how they are used as weapons. First of all, we should be clear about just how dangerous they are.

WEAPONS OF MASS DESTRUCTION

Biological weapons are, pound for pound, far more lethal than either nuclear or chemical weapons. Their killing potential is only exceeded by the most powerful nuclear weapons, i.e. H-bombs. An official American study compared the numbers of dead that would result from an attack with a nuclear weapon the size of the Hiroshima bomb (i.e. an explosive power equivalent to 12.5 kilotons of TNT), 300 kg of sarin nerve gas or 30 kg of anthrax spores. The bomb would kill between 23,000 and 80,000 people; the nerve gas, 60 to 200; the anthrax, 30,000 to 100,000. These estimates were worked out on the basis of a neither best nor worst case scenarios. The study points out that if conditions were more favourable to chemical and biological warfare, those weapons would kill even more.[2]

The difference between the lethality of biological and chemical weapons is huge. According to Dr Jonathan Tucker, then of the US Arms Control and Disarmament Agency, "Inhalation of only about eight thousand spores of anthrax bacteria, weighing less than a hundredth of a microgram [and a microgram is a millionth of a gram], results in an illness that is almost 100 percent fatal within five days. This compares with an inhaled lethal dose for the nerve agent sarin of about a milligram, or about one hundred thousand times greater. As a result, ten grams of anthrax spores, efficiently disseminated, could theoretically cause as many casualties as a metric ton of sarin."[3]

Biological weapons are cheap, too. As we saw in Chapter 1, the cost of the casualties they cause is a tiny fraction of those from conventional or nuclear weapons or nerve gases.

Anthrax is one of the most useful agents for biological weapons. However, there are at least 20 to 30 agents that could be used against human beings. They are caused by various sorts of micro-organisms.

CAUSATIVE MICRO-ORGANISMS

Viruses are the simplest sort of micro-organisms. They are unable to reproduce by themselves but they colonise other cells, reprogramming them to produce more viruses. Some viruses spread when we cough or sneeze; others in blood or other body fluids.

In people, viruses cause colds, AIDS, herpes, chicken pox, flu, polio, hepatitis, yellow fever, smallpox, dengue fever and various sorts of encephalitis. In animals, they are responsible for foot-and-mouth disease in cattle, sheep and pigs, canine distemper, rabies, African swine fever, Newcastle disease in poultry, Rift Valley fever in cattle, sheep and goats, and vesicular stomatitis in cattle, horses and pigs. In plants they cause mosaic diseases in tobacco, tomatoes and soybeans, and sugar-beet curly top.

Bacteria are free-living organisms. Made up of only one cell, they are the smallest organisms which can reproduce themselves. Some types of bacteria can transform themselves into spores—a form which is more resistant than usual to heat, cold and other environmental stresses. In general, bacteria cause illness either by invading tissues or by producing toxins. Some do both. Bacteria can be killed by antibiotics.

Bacterial toxins include botulinum, ricin, tetanus, diphtheria, shiga (which causes dysentery) and staphylococcus enterotoxin (food poisoning). Bacterial diseases include anthrax, brucellosis, cholera, glanders, melioidosis, pneumonic plague, tularemia and typhoid. These diseases have been considered as anti-personnel rather than anti-animal biological weapons, although the British also developed anthrax to attack cattle during World War II. In plants, bacteria cause rice and corn blight.

Rickettsia are a sort of mid-way between viruses and bacteria. They are bacteria but can only live inside host cells, like viruses. They are carried by insects such as lice, ticks, mice and fleas. Like bacteria, they are sensitive to antibiotics. In people, rickettsia cause typhus, Q-fever, psittacosis and Rocky Mountain spotted fever. In animals, rickettsia cause heart-water in sheep and goats.

Fungi are larger and more complex than bacteria. They reproduce by forming spores. In people, fungi cause coccidioidomycosis, an infection of the upper respiratory tract or lung. In animals: fungi produce a mycotoxin (aflatoxin) which causes the respiratory disease aspergillosis in poultry. In plants, fungi cause late blight in potato (which caused the Irish potato famine), black stem rust in cereals, and rice blast.

These lists of diseases are by no means the only ones caused by the various micro-organisms. They are the ones most commonly considered as biological warfare agents. But not all of them are equally suitable for weapons.

SUITABILITY

In order for a micro-organism to be suitable for use in biological war, a low dose of it should consistently produce a certain effect with a predictable incubation period. It must be able to survive, when disseminated, long enough to reach its target. The target population should have little or no immunity, and no access to treatment. The user should be able to protect his own troops and civilians. And the agent must be capable of mass production, stable storage and efficient dissemination.[4]

What then are the agents most commonly cited as suitable for biological warfare, and what effects would they have? Chapter 5 describes how scientific developments will increase the numbers of agents suitable for use as biological weapons. While this is a worrying prospect, the traditional agents are quite enough to cause alarm. The following ones do not depend on any new science. They exist in nature and have been either weaponised or researched for biological weapons for as long as programmes have existed. They could be used against people, animals and plants.[5]

AGAINST PEOPLE

The first five agents listed below were weaponised and stockpiled by the United States before the Biological Weapons Convention was negotiated in 1972.

Anthrax is a disease which affects herbivorous animals but which can also infect people. The bacteria (*Bacillus anthacis*) can be introduced through the skin (in a cut, for example), or through eating infected meat, or inhaled into the lungs. The cutaneous (skin) form results in huge black blisters and, if untreated with antibiotics, will result in death in 20 percent of cases. Pulmonary anthrax is far more serious but needs a higher dose to develop. It results in toxaemia and septicaemia and death within 48 hours in almost 100 percent of cases. A vaccine has been developed but its efficacy against a heavy dose of pulmonary anthrax is unknown. Antibiotics can be effective if the patient has previously been vaccinated, but must be given within a few hours of the onset of symptoms. The bacteria, which are easily produced in bulk, form spores which are resistant to heat and light and persist in the environment for decades. These spores would be sprayed in an aerosol if anthrax were to be used most effectively as a weapon.

Tularemia is found in rodents, rabbits and hares. The causative agent (*Francisella tularensis)* can infect people through insect bites, contaminated water or food or by being breathed into the lungs. It is extremely contagious: one bacterium is enough. After an incubation period of 2–3 days the symptoms are similar to pneumonia, and mortality varies according to the type of bacteria. It is highest—up to 40 percent—in the United States. A vaccine is available, and recovery confers life-long immunity. The bacteria are easily produced and persist in the environment.

Brucellosis is an incapacitating disease which humans can catch from goats, cattle and pigs, usually by eating contaminated meat or milk. The patient is feverish for between a month and a year, and relapses can occur for several years. Mortality is low: between 2 and 5 percent. There is no human vaccine.

Q-fever is also incapacitating. It is caused in humans by a bacterium called *Coxiella burnetii* which is carried by many animals. After an incubation period of 2–3 weeks the patient develops a high temperature, intense headache and pneumonia. The mortality rate is low—1–4 percent of cases—but the agent is hardy and very little of it is necessary to cause the disease. Vaccination is available.

Venezuelan equine encephalomyelitis is mainly a disease of horses, but insects can transfer it to people. After an incubation period of 4–20 days, it causes an influenza-type illness which lasts for up to a week. Mortality is low, but the causative virus is stable in an aerosol and highly infectious to humans when delivered by this route. A vaccine is available.

These agents were stockpiled by the US military before being destroyed between 1971 and 1973. Another agent studied by the US in the 1950s is *Yersinia pestis*, the rod-shaped bacterium which causes bubonic or pneumonic plague. The bubonic form is transmitted by fleas carried by rats. The pneumonic form results from breathing the organisms in, and as they would almost certainly be delivered in aerosol form, pneumonic plague would most likely result from a biological warfare attack. After an incubation period of two or three days, victims cough blood and develop pneumonia with high temperatures, chills and muscle pain. Harsh, labored breathing and death quickly follow. The condition is practically always fatal if antibiotics are not given within 24 hours of the onset of symptoms. There is no effective vaccine against pneumonic plague.

Yellow fever is caused by a virus normally spread by mosquitoes. It is highly infectious in aerosol form. After an incubation period of three to six days, the disease begins with fever, muscle aches, headache and nausea, and progresses through jaundice and black vomit to death in between 20 and 70 percent of cases. Vaccination is widely available. People who survive are immune, but epidemics occur in populations who lack immunity.

AGAINST ANIMALS

These agents have not produced as much military interest as those against people, but the Americans studied all the following ones intensively during World War II. This was also when the British prepared for attacks against German cattle, although with anthrax rather than the agents listed below.

Foot-and-mouth is a highly contagious disease of cloven-hoofed animals (cattle, pigs, sheep etc.). After an incubation period of 2–8 days, infected animals develop painful ulcers that last for up to 10 days on the tongue, lips and feet. The disease causes large production losses and may kill up to 50 percent of calves affected. The virus which causes it is hardy and persists in eg hay for weeks or months.

Newcastle disease affects birds and is also highly contagious. The incubation period is generally 5–6 days, after which a variety of symptoms can include loss of appetite, plummeting egg production, green diarrhoea and dehydration. Mortality can exceed 90 percent.

Heart-water affects ruminants (cattle, water buffalo, sheep, goats etc.) and is carried by ticks. It occurs mainly in Africa, south of the Sahara. The incubation period is 2–4 weeks, after which infected animals develop high fever and can die within a week. Mortality can be as high as 100 percent.

AGAINST PLANTS

Staple crops are targets for economic warfare. The first two of the following agents were stockpiled but not weaponised by the United States. All have been studied as potential BW agents.

Rice blast is caused by a fungus (*Pyricularia oryzae*) which survives in a variety of ways, depending on climate, and can be widely disseminated. It causes small, bluish flecks on the leaves which rapidly enlarge and may kill entire leaves. The number of rice grains that mature is reduced, and yield loss can be as high as 60 percent.

Black stem rust attacks cereals—wheat, barley, oats and rye—and causes crop losses of up to 90 percent. The fungus (*Puccinia graminis tritici*) that causes it in wheat forms huge amounts of spores which can be blown for enormous distances: eg 4,000 km from the west to the east of Australia. Both for black stem rust and for rice blast, computer programmes have been developed to try to predict the spread of the disease, to help farmers combat it. Understanding the genetics of resistance in rice and wheat has been another line of defence against it and rice blast.

Sugar beet curly top is a disease of herbaceous plants which devastates sugar beet, bean and tomato. It is spread by a leafhopper, which transmits the causative virus when it feeds. Resistant varieties of sugar beet, bean and tomato have been developed.

Bacterial blight of rice is widespread in Asia where it reduces yields by up to 30 percent. It is carried by wind, rain or insects, and causes infected leaves to turn yellow and wither. Again, resistant strains of rice have been developed.

TOXINS

The first two listed below were weaponised by the United States after the Second World War; the third was produced there in developmental quantities during the War.

Botulinum toxins are the most toxic compounds known. A mere thousandth of a millionth of a gram per kilogram of body weight of the type called strain A is enough to kill a human being, making it 15,000 times more toxic than the nerve gas VX and 100,000 times more toxic than the nerve gas sarin. Produced by the bacterium *Clostridium botulinum,* the toxin is a white crystalline substance that readily dissolves in water when finely powdered. It could be used in an aerosol attack (although it decays in air and quickly loses much of its toxicity), or to contaminate food in which it causes the poisoning known as botulism. Symptoms begin with nausea, diarrhoea, dizziness and weakness, and progress through double vision, choking mucus and laboured breathing to convulsions and death. If given before the onset of symptoms (i.e. before 24 hours has elapsed), an antitoxin is effective against inhaled botulinum.

Staphylococcal enterotoxin B is an extremely toxic incapacitant, low doses of which cause poisoning which lasts for one to two weeks. Most patients would recover, but the toxin can be lethal. It is relatively stable in aerosol form and could also be ingested in food, or freeze-dried to produce a white, fluffy material that dissolves easily in water—making it suitable for poisoning small volume water supplies. Three to twelve hours after inhaling the toxin, victims suddenly develop fever, headache, chills, a cough, nausea, vomiting and diarrhoea. There is no human vaccination against *SEB* but several candidates are in development.

Shellfish poison, sometimes known as saxitoxin, is made by certain algae (eg some types of plankton). Shellfish that feed on them are very poisonous. People who eat the shellfish develop symptoms 10 minutes-4 hours afterwards: tingling numbness in the mouth, muscular weakness, decreasing muscular co-ordination, paralysis and death. The toxin is easily produced and is soluble in water. Estimates of the lethal dose via ingestion range from 0.2 mg to 4 mg; but only one-tenth of this is necessary for death by injection. In that case—say on a rifle-fired flechette which can penetrate the skin with a hardly noticeable sting—death can occur in 15 minutes.

Ricin is made from castor beans. In its crystalline form its toxicity is about the same as saxitoxin. Its effect is delayed by 12 to 24 hours, but it produces fever, collapse in blood pressure and death.

FROM AGENTS TO WEAPONS

All of the agents considered above have to be made into weapons before they can be used in biological warfare. The types of weapons used depend on the way the disease is spread.

Spreading disease

As the lists above reveal, there are several ways of spreading these agents of disease. They may be dispersed in the atmosphere, added to food or water, or injected by objects or by insects. Whatever the method, they must first be stabilised in liquid suspensions or alternatively freeze dried and kept in powdered form.[6]

When biological weapons were first being developed, they were dispersed into the air in an aerosol produced when a bomb exploded. This is still an option—Saddam Hussein of Iraq had such weapons ready to fire in the 1991 Gulf War, for example. Aerosols can also be produced by spray units which can be fitted to aircraft if a large area is to be covered or can be as small as paint or even scent sprayers for a localised attack. As Dr Graham Pearson has pointed out: "We need to always remember that effective dissemination can be achieved through relatively simple spray systems. A simple paint sprayer can produce particles of the right size very effectively."[7]

The effect actually obtained depends on various factors. To begin with, the particles of agent have to survive their journey to the lung. Different particles have different sensitivities, but some will be killed in the explosion if they are dispersed from a bomb, or in a sprayer. Many factors affect their survival: temperature, light, humidity and air pollutants. Unsuitable weather can severely reduce the effect of aerosolised agents. Clear nights with little wind are reckoned to be best: they allow the aerosol cloud to remain reasonably concentrated. There is then more chance that anyone caught in it will breathe in the required dose. For this is another factor that has to be taken into account: the agent will only cause the condition if enough of it is taken in. Different diseases need different doses because biological agents vary in their ability to cause illness or death. Half of one ounce of botulinal toxin would in principle be enough to kill 350 million people, although in practice its loss of toxicity in an aerosol would reduce its lethality.[8] The lethal dose of anthrax spores—about eight thousand—would easily fit on the full stop at the end of this sentence. One gram of anthrax could, if distributed effectively, kill more than 100 million people. In practice, of course, it would not be distributed optimally and would not kill nearly this number. Other diseases need fewer bacteria: one single bacterium can cause tularemia.[9]

Agents will inevitably die or lose their virulence when they are released into the atmosphere. World Health Organisation experts have estimated different decay rates for different agents in an aerosol cloud. If the agents have been produced in a special way to protect them from environmental conditions, the experts predict that the agents that cause Q-fever will decay at a rate of 10 percent per minute; those that cause yellow fever at 30 percent per minute; tularemia and plague, 2 percent per minute; and anthrax, 0.1 percent per minute.

The particles also have to be the right size to be breathed in and kept in the lungs: between 1 and 5 microns (1–5 millionths of a metre) is most efficient. Aerosolisation is the most difficult (if also the most dangerous) way of spreading agent; but the difficulties are not necessarily thought to be insuperable.

Contaminating food and water

The second means of administering biological agents is by adding them to food or water. The virus which causes foot-and-mouth disease in cattle, say, could be fed to them on hay. People's food can be poisoned with micro-organisms which attack the digestive organs (eg *Salmonella*). A phial of these agents could be added to food during production, distribution or other parts of the consumer chain. Nearly all micro-organisms are destroyed by heat, but if they are added later in the production process the food provides a good environment for them to survive and for some to produce toxins. Food poisoning can be immediately incapacitating—attested to by airline crews having to eat different meals—and even fatal. In 1996, the bacterium E.coli 0157 was blamed for outbreaks of food poisoning in Japan, where it killed 11 people and made another 10,000 ill, and Scotland, where it killed 17 people and made more than 100 ill.

Urban water supplies in developed countries are less vulnerable than might be thought to contamination. Although reservoirs contaminated with disease-causing agents could theoretically poison large sections of populations, they are in fact largely protected not only with chlorine and filters, but by the sheer volume of water they supply. Any agent added would be so diluted as to probably cause little harm. Smaller volume supplies, as well as untreated supplies and wells, are more vulnerable.

Transmitting disease

Some infections are carried by insects: bubonic plague by fleas, spotted typhus by fleas and lice, malaria by mosquitoes. These then are another possible way of dispersing biological agents. In this case the weapon is a container for the insects plus a delivery system for taking them to the target area. The difficulties of making sure that the insects find their targets make this an unreliable method, but it could still have large effects. A computer simulation[10] imagines a fishing boat with a crew of three men rescuing some refugees, who die from exposure before the boat reaches port. Unknown to the crew, the refugees have been infected with bubonic plague but have not yet shown symptoms. The crew, who are bitten by the plague-carrying fleas, carry the infection back to their village of 400 people. In six days, 250 villagers have come down with the disease.

An agent will infect the largest number of people if it is aerosolised, and national programmes have concentrated on this method of dispersion. So far, non-national groups have not been able to straddle the hurdles that aerosolisation sets up, and they have found it most effective to introduce the agent to the victim directly, either injecting it or contaminating food. But this state of affairs is not expected to last. This is why the terrorist threat is becoming so real; and it is to this we turn in the next chapter.

3

TERRORISM

There was nothing unusual about the crowds hurrying to work in the Tokyo rush hour on the morning of 20 March, 1995. In the tube system, orderly streams of people negotiated the escalators and underground halls to arrive at their platforms and be pushed onto the trains. Among the commuters, however, were five whose job was to be done during, rather than after, their journeys. They were members of the apocalyptic religious sect Aum Shinrikyo; and their mission was to kill as many of their fellow passengers as possible.

The five terrorists caught trains on the Hibiya, Marunouchi and Chiyoda lines which were all due to arrive at Kasumigaseki station between 8.09 and 8.13 A.M. Above this station lie a concentration of government offices: The Ministries of Foreign Affairs, Home Affairs, Health and Welfare, Agriculture, Labour and several others. The terrorists' aim was to bring death and panic right to the heart of the state.

The sect members carried parcels wrapped in brown paper. Once on board, they put them under their seats and used the tips of their umbrellas to punch holes in them. From the packages, lethal sarin gas escaped into the carriages. Only a very faint smell warned of what was to come. After about 15 seconds, nearby passengers felt the first effects: tightness in the chest; difficulty in breathing; pain in the eyes; dimming vision. One, Akio Masahata, recalls: "It hurt to breathe. I could feel it in my nostrils. People were starting to collapse around me."[1] They fell, giddy, sweating, vomiting, belching, urinating and defecating involuntarily. Some succumbed to convulsions and death.

Panic ensued. At the next station, gasping people groped for the doors. They reeled, tottered onto the platforms. Staggered towards the station exits, many falling on the way. Emergency medical teams arrived. People were stretchered out, vomiting, bubbles coming from their mouths, blood from their noses.

Twelve people died; 5,500 were injured, some permanently. If the terrorists had not used a faulty batch of sarin, and had disseminated it more effectively, their attack could have killed tens of thousands of people.

This was an attack with a chemical weapon: a nerve gas. It was not the first the cult had attempted. In June, 1994, they had killed seven people with sarin in a night attack in Matsumoto, a small mountain resort north of Tokyo. But the Aum Shinrikyo were developing biological weapons as well. The police found they had 160 barrels of media for growing *Clostridium botulinum* bacteria, which produces botulinus toxin. They had already tried out spreading some of this round Tokyo, but without effect. In 1990 and 1993 they had tried to spray the toxin from a vehicle driving around the national parliament and the centre of the city; and they had also experimented with anthrax spores which they sprayed from the roof of an eight-storey building in eastern Tokyo. That killed birds but no people. A US Senate committee alleges that cult members had also tried to obtain the Ebola virus—which causes a particularly horrifying infection, in which the body disintegrates in pools of blood—from Zaire.[2]

The motive for the attack was as bizarre as the cult itself. Documents in Aum files found by the police predicted that the world would undergo a major cataclysm by 1997, and that at least 90 percent of people in major cities would die—some in gas attacks. The cult was evidently working to bring these prophecies about.

The Tokyo attack was a psychological watershed. The Aum had done what was known to be possible but presumed to be beyond the pale. The unthinkable had happened. Given the interest already shown by other groups in biological terrorism, the ease of acquisition of biological materials, the difficulty of detecting them, and their capacity to inflict terror, many feared that it might happen again.

INCREASING THREAT

The increasing terrorist threat is causing concern amongst experts. In the past few years terrorists have set off massive explosions at a federal building in Oklahoma City and the New York World Trade

Center. Again, these were directed towards civilians. The attackers at the World Trade Center tried to release cyanide gas which was meant to kill everyone trapped in one of the towers. At the subsequent trial, one of the judges said this was thwarted only because the sodium cyanide burned instead of vaporising. It is only a short step from this to a BW dimension to attacks like these. They would add terror and put extra strain on public authorities. "Visualize the World Trade Center or an Oklahoma-style attack complicated by the inclusion of a kilogram of anthrax spores as a kind of microbiological shrapnel along with the explosives," suggests Nobel-Prize winning geneticist Joshua Lederberg. "[Imagine] its implications for salvage and rescue, public health, panic."[3] The US Central Intelligence Agency is expecting "a tremendous increase" in terrorism over the next ten years: "rogue nations, terrorists, subnational groups, cells of ethnic or religious zealots, even individuals with a grudge, are expected to attempt mass urban panic and destruction with . . . widely accessible chemical and biological agents."[4] The breakdown of state structures in the former Soviet Union, the increasing economic distress of scientists there who may be tempted to sell their expertise abroad, the rise of ethnic conflicts—all these developments increase the number of non-state entities which may want to attack others, and be able to develop or hire the know-how. And the fact that biological agents generally take time to have an effect is advantageous for terrorists. By that time, they can be far away.

THREATS TO FOOD AND AGRICULTURE

These have hardly begun to be taken seriously at official level. A conference of experts held in Georgetown, Washington in September 1998, concluded that "terrorism against agriculture and the US food supply has largely been ignored as a threat." Yet the US food and fiber system accounts for 13 percent of the country's Gross Domestic Product and 17 percent of its employment. Terrorist attacks on food and agriculture would not only disrupt domestic food supplies but the economy too. The last major foreign animal disease outbreak in the US was of avian influenza in 1983–84. It was confined to Pennsylvania and neighbouring states, but over the course of six months, all chickens there had to be killed and all premises decontaminated. The cost was $63 million—the most expensive eradication effort in US history. The US also exports food to the value of $140 billion each year. If it were known to be contaminated with a disease, the loss of these markets would eliminate the country's budget surplus.

The conference, which was organised by the National Consortium for Genomic Resources Management and Services (GenCon),[5] heard that farming is increasingly concentrating animals in specific areas, which reduces the target area for a terrorist, increases the potential for the spread of infectious agents and magnifies the impact of limited use. Diseases affecting animals and crops could be introduced by tourists, travellers or terrorists. Yet although the counter-terrorism community is committing resources to tackling bioterrorism against people (see below), it is blind to the threat to agriculture. The meeting urged the setting up of a national system to try to protect food and agricultural resources.

PREVIOUS THREATS

Joseph Stalin considered assassinating Joseph Broz Tito by disseminating plague bacteria at a reception. The attack never took place. There have been plenty of other incidents in which groups of various hues have been found in possession of biological agents.[6]

- In 1972, members of a right-wing group known as "Order of the Rising Sun" were arrested in Chicago with between 30 and 40 kg of typhoid bacteria cultures which they were going to use to poison water supplies in Chicago, St Louis and other cities in the Midwest. Their obsession was the creation of a new master race.
- In September 1984, members of the Rajneesh cult contaminated salad bars in The Dalles, Oregon, with *Salmonella typhi*, which causes typhoid fever. They were trying to influence the outcome of a local election. Nobody was killed but 750 people became ill.
- A US tax protest group called "The Patriots Council" were convicted in February 1995 of possessing 0.7 grams of the toxin ricin—enough to kill 100 people. They had been planning to poison US government agents by smearing ricin on their doorknobs.

- A mere six weeks after the Tokyo attack, Larry Harris, who belongs to a white supremacist group called Aryan Nations, called the American Type Culture Collection in Maryland and ordered three vials of freeze-dried bacteria, *Y. pestis,* that cause pneumonic and bubonic plague. They were duly delivered by Federal Express; but while they were in transit Harris became impatient and called again to ask why they had not arrived. His manner made the supplier suspicious enough to notify federal authorities, and Harris was charged with mail fraud. Had he sat tight and waited, he would not have been caught.

Against the background of these and other incidents, it is hardly surprising that a five-month study by the US Senate concluded, in March 1996, that "the threat of a terrorist group using a nuclear, biological or chemical weapon of mass destruction in the United States is real. It is not a matter of 'if' but rather 'when' such an event will occur."[7]

Discoveries of biological attacks have not been limited to the United States. A Red Army Faction safe house in Paris was found to contain a bathtub of botulinal toxin in the 1980s; and in 1994, Prince Mikasa of Japan admitted that Japanese military officials had laced fruit with cholera germs to try to poison the members of the 1931 League of Nations Lytton Commission, who were investigating the seizure of Manchuria.

Seth Carus of the National Defense University in Washington has made an exhaustive study of bioterrorism. He has chronicled 52 confirmed cases this century in which terrorists, criminals or others expressed interest in biological agents, threatened to use them, attempted to acquire them, or possessed or used them. The cases, which resulted in 982 victims, including nine deaths, were intended to achieve various ends: murder, extortion, incapacitation, mass murder, terror, making a political statement, and revenge. They excluded states acting as terrorists (eg the Bulgarian Secret Police's assassination of Georgi Markov).

His prognosis is not comforting. "The available evidence indicates that there is an explosion of interest by criminals in biological agents," he writes. "There is also reason for concern that future bioterrorism attacks may be more deadly than past incidents.

Three factors account for the change. First, an increasing number of terrorist groups—foreign and domestic—are adopting the tactic of inflicting mass casualties to achieve ideological, revenge or 'religious' goals . . . Second, the technological sophistication of the terrorist groups is growing . . . Finally, Aum Shinrikyo demonstrated that terrorist groups now exist with resources comparable to some governments. Therefore, it is increasingly likely that some group will become capable of using biological agents to cause massive casualties."

HOW EASY TO MAKE?

Terrorist weapons need not perform efficiently to produce the desired effect. The Aum's sarin was impure and the means of delivery was crude; yet that attack may have changed the face of terrorism. Terrorists want to demonstrate their power to cause panic and death in the face of the authorities; and they can achieve that with fewer deaths than their equipment is theoretically capable of producing. Their weapons do not have to be good—just good enough.

Even the Iraqi's biological weapons were not sophisticated. Microbiologist Raymond Zilinskas, of the University of Maryland Biotechnology Institute, participated in the United Nations' search for Iraqi weapons after the Gulf War. "The Iraqis never mastered the art of weaponising their bacterial agents, which included anthrax," he says. "Most of what the UN investigators found were crude preparations mounted on conventional bombs and missiles, which might not have dispersed very well."[8] But Zilinskas confirms that crude weapons can be effective. According to him, a slurry of anthrax spores left in the tunnels of an underground railway system, where they would be dried and blown around by the wind created by the passing trains, could kill thousands of people. The Iraqis could also have concealed a more sophisticated BW facility from the UN inspectors. They certainly concealed a lot, as we shall see in Chapter 4.

According to Carus, it has never been difficult for terrorists or criminals to gain access to biological agents. They have bought them from legitimate suppliers, stolen them, produced them themselves or used materials taken from nature which have been contaminated with them. Anthrax, plague, brucellosis and tularemia are all obtainable from natural sources in the environment. The spores of anthrax, for example, which persist for decades, could be collected from soil samples in areas where the disease is endemic in cattle; and the same could be done with brucellosis. Ricin can be extracted from castor beans: yields are typically about one gram of toxin per kilogram of seeds.[9] Tricothecene mycotoxins can be extracted from corn and aflatoxin from peanuts.

Once obtained, bacteria can be grown into larger quantities quite simply: they grow very happily in a flask of chicken soup. Viruses may be less favoured because they generally do not live long outside a host; but they do proliferate when injected into an ordinary hen's egg. One author rates the process of producing lethal biological agents as "about as complicated as manufacturing beer and less dangerous than refining heroin."[10] And Kathleen Bailey, formerly of the US Arms Control and Disarmament Agency, is "absolutely convinced" that "a major biological arsenal could be built in a room 15-by-15 feet, with £5,000 worth of equipment."[11]

The terrorist would, of course, have to have some knowledge of biology and some technical skill. There is a spread of estimates of the level of education needed, from college students to postgraduates. According to Lt Col Terry N. Mayer of the US Air Force, "If an attacker has access to the target area, a simple mechanism to aerosolise a substance, and a basic biology laboratory, the prerequisites are complete. This is not a high-tech arena that requires specialised equipment or core material . . . ; this is basic college biology coupled with motivation."[12] Other experts reckon postgraduate expertise would be necessary. The Aum cult is reported to have included scientists and engineers. It was a sophisticated and wealthy group, reported to have amassed at least $300 million in assets and recruited 10,000 members.

Under optimal conditions, many types of bacteria can divide every 20 minutes. That means that one bacterium can become 1,074,000,000 after ten hours.[13] Even with a crude system such as a fish tank, a terrorist could make a slurry containing billions of spores. The slurry could be spread in liquid form using a sprayer, although it may clog the nozzles, and a large percentage of agent spread in this way generally dies as it is sprayed. (This might explain why the Aum had so little success with its attempts to spray agent around Tokyo.) It is much easier to spread dry agent—perhaps freeze-dried—but this would be a dangerous process.

The biotechnology industry uses freeze-dryers, which preserve materials by freezing them and putting them under a vacuum to remove moisture. The most dangerous part of the operation would be grinding the slurry powder into particles of the right size. The terrorists would have to use some safety techniques to avoid infecting themselves. Either way, aerosolisation is complicated; but it would be foolish to rule out the possibility that it could be done. And even if it were done sub-optimally, that could still be enough for terrorist purposes.

Nobody disputes that laboratory workers can grow and handle biological agents in moderately well-equipped laboratories. There is more disagreement about terrorists' ability to handle some of the most dangerous pathogens known. In view of reports that the Japanese Aum sect had tried to collect samples of the Ebola virus, it is interesting to ask whether such a group could feasibly work with such an organism.

There is no treatment and no cure for Ebola. It is contagious, although just how contagious is not yet clear. While there is no evidence of airborne transmission, epidemiological studies show that it is passed on through blood and infectious body fluids, in the same way as the AIDS virus; so close contact with another person can lead to infection. Compared with influenza or measles, however, it is quite hard to catch.

Expert opinions about whether a terrorist group could handle such a virus are disconcerting. Dr Graham Lloyd is Head of Diagnosis at the UK's Centre for Microbiology and Applied Research (CAMR) at Porton Down. The site used to be part of the UK biological defence effort, but CAMR is part of the public health sector which reports to the Department of Health. It devotes itself to health care research. Graham Lloyd works in the most secure conditions yet devised to handle and diagnose dangerous viruses like Ebola—so-called P4 level containment laboratories. The viruses are handled either in a series of interconnected cabinets or in laboratories in which personnel wear highly specialised protective suits that look like space suits (and have their own external air supply). The laboratory design, construction and safety practices ensure no escape of the agents to the community at large. It has its own filtered air supply and is heavily restricted to experienced personnel. Before entering, they must decontaminate under showers. They must work in pairs when they handle an agent. The air pressure in the entire laboratory is kept lower than that outside, so that if any agent escapes it will be sucked back into the lab rather than float out.

Graham Lloyd has considered whether a terrorist group could manipulate Ebola without such security: "They could, if they had access to the agent, microbiological skills and wanted to take the risk working in less secure environments."[14] In his opinion, however, there would be a high risk of disease, and clinical cases would easily be recognised by vigilant health professionals.

Dr Graham Pearson, former director of the UK's chemical and biological defence research, warns against being taken in by the western mindset. This, he says, assumes that if protective security measures are available, they are necessary. "In the UK now we'd never dream of handling Ebola in less than P4. We'd only work with anthrax in P3 [one grade less of laboratory security] or, if it's aerosolised, P4. But during World War II the UK produced cattle cakes containing anthrax, and the people doing this put anthrax spores into the centre of the cakes without wearing respirators. They worked in a little shed behind a sheet of glass. One person got subcutaneous anthrax, treatable with penicillin. If you took care, it didn't spread. Also the United Nations teams investigating Iraq's BW potential found that they would work on micro-organisms in straightforward cabinets."[15]

This may beg the question of how contagious the micro-organisms are. Anthrax is not contagious. Ebola is more so. Yet working with it in less than ideal conditions would not horrify Jeffrey Almond, Professor in the School of Animal and Microbial Sciences at the University of Reading. You would, he says, need good microbiological technique, and work with the right air-flow. "If you were careful, there'd be no reason to get infected."[16] Given these views, and that suicide terrorists have already shown themselves ready to die for their causes, blowing themselves up with their victims, it is obviously not farfetched to imagine sophisticated cults like the Aum being willing to take the risk.

GOVERNMENT MEASURES

In December 1995, 54-year old American citizen Thomas Lewis Lavy hanged himself in his prison cell. He had been found by Canadian customs officials to be carrying 130 grams of ricin—enough to kill 32,000 people, according to the FBI. He claimed he had bought the poison in Canada to poison coyotes that were killing chickens on his farm in Arkansas, but he was also found to have neo-Nazi literature. He was prosecuted under the US Biological Weapons Anti-Terrorism Act of 1989, which has proved a successful vehicle for prosecuting some people found with dangerous agents.

Since this legislation was passed, the attacks in Tokyo and in the US have concentrated government minds on the problem of terrorism. Presidential Decision Directive 39, issued in June 1995, declared: "Terrorist acquisition of weapons of mass destruction is not acceptable and there is no higher priority than preventing the acquisition of such materials/weapons or removing this capability from terrorist groups." A few months later, a Senate report pointed out the particular areas in which the US needed to improve. It asserted that the US was not properly prepared to respond to terrorists with weapons of mass destruction. "Much improvement is necessary in support of our country's "first responders"—local fire, police, rescue and emergency room personnel. Government efforts need to be better co-ordinated, and the intelligence and law enforcement communities must make greater strides in information-sharing."[17] These concerns found Congressional backing in the Nunn-Lugar-Domenici legislation, passed in September 1996 in the wake of an attack against an American base in Saudi Arabia, which created the Domestic Preparedness programme to provide training to 120 cities in how to respond to chemical and biological incidents.

In April 1996, President Clinton signed the Antiterrorism and Effective Death Penalty Act which strengthened previous legislation in the field.[18] Part of it is concerned with making the transfer of hazardous agents safer. The Centers for Disease Control and Prevention (CDC) in Atlanta has since drawn up stricter rules for this, which came into effect in April 1997.

Under the CDC's new regime, mavericks like Larry Harris can no longer order up dangerous pathogens. Most facilities that handle these micro-organisms, whether commercial suppliers, government agencies, universities, research institutions or private companies, will have to be inspected to see they can handle them properly, and registered. Permission will have to be given and recorded for every transfer of an agent. The scheme is "designed to ensure that select agents are not shipped to parties who are not equipped to handle them appropriately or who otherwise lack proper authorisation for their requests."[19] There are some exemptions for clinical laboratories, so that the work of scientists there will not be hampered. All the major bacteria, viruses, rickettsiae, fungi and toxins which are generally cited in connection with BW are covered by the new rules.

The new regime will make it more difficult for terrorists to obtain micro-organisms, but it will not stop them. According to Michael Moodie, President of the Chemical and Biological Arms Control Institute, "It will not make much difference with respect to classical biological agents. Anthrax is not hard to find. You don't have to go to the CDC to get cultures."[20] Terrorists will still be able to steal them, order them from abroad, or cultivate them from natural sources.

Much less information is available about the UK government's anti-terrorist efforts. The Home Office is responsible for counter-terrorism. All it is willing to say is that it has "developed over a period of years, a series of contingency plans for responding to a wide range of terrorist threats, including those which might involve the threatened or actual use of nuclear, chemical or biological materials. The Government is firmly committed to ensuring that the country has the necessary plans in place in the interests of national security and the protection of the public. These plans are regularly reviewed, tested and updated in the light of changing domestic and international circumstances."[21] It is not willing to divulge anything about the plans themselves, except that, as with civil emergencies in general, operational control of any incident would be a matter for the Chief Officer of Police in whose area the offence was committed.

The UK has passed the 1974 Biological Weapons Act to prohibit any person or group possessing suspect biological agents or developing biological weapons. The penalty for these offences is life imprisonment. There have not been any prosecutions under the Act. In July 1998, the UK government published a White Paper[22] on strategic export controls, proposing that regulations on biological weapons should be as stringent as those on chemical weapons. This would mean that it would be an offence for anyone in the UK or a UK person abroad to enlist the aid of a foreigner overseas to develop, procure or use a biological weapon. In addition, it suggests making publication of technology subject to export controls an offence, in an effort to reach people publishing on the internet.

Several international legal measures also exist to fight terrorism. The International Convention for the Suppression of Terrorist Bombings opened for signature in January 1999, and specifically applies to biological and toxin agents. In July 1998, 120 states signed an agreement to set up an International Criminal Court which will be able to try people accused of violating laws governing conduct in war, such as the Genocide Convention.

Many states have not passed similar legislation to outlaw biological terrorism on their soil. The Japanese government, for example, had no law which would have given it the power to investigate the Aum group's activities to the extent needed to stop them before the attack on the Tokyo underground. In spite of government efforts to deal with the problem, the actual and feared growth in terrorist activities is one of the main dynamos powering the increasing threat of biological weapons.

If terrorists can make crude biological weapons, so can many states. Iraq's secret programme brings home the threat of proliferation of biological weapons; and it is to that we now turn.

FIRE STORM

"Fire Storm," an emergency planning exercise in Greater Manchester, swung into action on Friday, 17 November, 1995. Police refused to confirm reports that it was a counter-BW scenario involving terrorists unleashing a canister of anthrax spores. "The press are not invited," commented one police officer. "It's private."

Official sources did however reveal that it was a large-scale exercise: so large that one officer predicted there would not be another similar one for the next 15 years. About 250 visiting police, security and government officials from round the country were among those taking part. It was reported that the Home Secretary, Michael Howard, followed the exercise from his desk in London.

The emergency planning authorities in Manchester conduct several exercises a year involving the police, fire, ambulance and health services. They use a geographical information system to pinpoint the putative release, and combine this with weather forecasts to predict the plume of chemical, biological or radiological pollution. The weather would influence the authorities' response to the release of a biological agent. Evacuation might be considered if there was little wind, in which case the agent would lie around and could pose a danger. If it was windy, the agent would be dispersed and people would be advised to take shelter where they were. The toxicity of the agent would also determine the advice given. Given the dangers of mass evacuation and panic, the authorities prefer to advise what they call "shelter in place" if it is feasible.

And operation "Fire Storm"?—was it practice for a biological release? One officer responded: "There is no publicly available information on that type of exercise."

WHAT IF?

Imagine it is some time during the year 2001, and the United Nations sanctions against Iraq, imposed after the Gulf War, are still in place. For the civilian population of Iraq, they have meant years of poverty, hunger, indignity, inadequate health care and rising infant mortality. Saddam Hussein has already discovered several attempts to overthrow him, and has murdered the plotters. He needs to unite the country behind him, to give him breathing space. The UN is about to hold its periodic review of the sanctions. Saddam Hussein decides to attack the two countries most keen to maintain them: the US and the UK.

At 1am on an overcast night with a moderate wind, a small boat casts off from its mooring on the Potomac River just north of Washington DC. Just above the Theodore Roosevelt Memorial it activates its aerosol generator, which releases 10 kg of anthrax spores as the boat passes downriver. The spores drift over the city. The boat reaches Chesapeake Bay and heads out into the Atlantic. By morning it has been scuttled, the crew having been lifted off by helicopter. Within five days, hundreds of thousands of people have died in Washington.

It is late in the afternoon of the same day in England, and first news of the catastrophe in Washington will not break for several more hours. The streets are crowded as people head home from work. A plane takes off from a southern airport and heads north, following a route to the west of London. There is a westerly crosswind blowing at 10 km per hour. As the plane crosses the Thames it turns on its aerosol sprays. The pilot knows that the bacteria he is releasing are delicate and that only 10 percent will survive in the spray, and that these will die off at a rate of 5 percent per minute. He also knows that a large proportion will be killed by the pollution generated by the city traffic. Nevertheless he is confident that hundreds of the people hurrying along London's streets will be infected with plague, and that these people will pass the disease on to hundreds more. After two or three days, when the only news is of the American crisis, the first London casualties collapse with high temperatures, chills and headaches. Plague is diagnosed; stocks of antibiotics are rushed to GP's and hospitals. Many of those who receive treatment within 24 hours of the onset of symptoms are saved. Thousands die within a week.

GRAPES OF WRATH

Imagine that a group of disgruntled European winemakers, angry that their profits are being squeezed by the increasing popularity of California wines, enter the US as tourists and take a trip round wine-producing counties in Northern California. Occasionally they stop their car and stroll up to look at the vineyards. At these stops they take tins of pate out of their pockets and scrape some onto the ground—pate that contains millions of grape aphids *(phylloxera vastratrix)* which will settle into the soil and attack the roots of the plants. Long after the Europeans have disappeared, the aphids will destroy as much as 70 percent of the vines. They breed prolifically—according to some estimates, one aphid can produce a staggering 48 *billion* offspring—and are carried by wind, water and in soil sticking to boots or vehicle wheels. The only way to eradicate them is by removing the vines and replanting aphid-resistant plants—at huge cost to the industry.

SABOTAGING WATER

It is not so easy to sabotage urban water supplies in technologically advanced countries as it might seem. These countries filter their water and add chlorine to kill micro-organisms. The sheer volume of water needed to supply a city would mean, according to a US Department of Defense biological warfare analyst, that somebody wanting to poison New York's supplies would need "trainloads" of botulinum toxin to overcome the dilution.

Where groundwater sources are pure enough to be distributed without additives, they are more vulnerable to sabotage. And wells have been poisoned in warfare for thousands of years.

DEADLY DOUGHNUTS

Early in the morning of 29 October, 1996, laboratory workers at St Paul Medical Center, Texas, were invited to sample pastries in their lunchroom. The invitation came via an e-mail message, and those who responded found two boxes of blueberry muffins and assorted doughnuts. Between 7.15 A.M. and 1.30 P.M., eleven employees enjoyed the treat; one took a muffin home to share that night.

At 9 P.M. that evening, the first pastry-eater suffered severe gastrointestinal illness. All were sick by 4am on 1 November. They had been infected with a particular type of *Shigella dysenteriae* that causes vomiting, diarrhoea, headache and fever. Of the twelve infected, four had to be hospitalised and five others were treated at emergency clinics. All survived.

Investigations showed that the laboratory kept the same type of *Shigella* and that some of its stock was missing. On 28 August, 1997, laboratory technician Diane Thompson was charged with poisoning the pastries. She was convicted in September 1998, and sentenced to 20 years in prison.

In November 1998, anthrax, plague and brucella were offered to reporters posing as middlemen for a medical laboratory in North Africa, who telephoned the Bio Farma research institute in Bandung, Indonesia.[22] For about £600 the institute was willing to send cultures of these organisms by mail-order, without any check on the identities of the buyers or what the organisms would be used for.

The reporters identified 450 laboratories world-wide which keep cultures of micro-organisms. Anthrax was sold by more than 50; botulinum by 34 and plague by 18. The journalists approached 20 at random. The Veterinary Research Institute in Brno, in the Czech Republic, was willing to sell botulinum for a mere £18–50. The reporters were told they could send a representative to pick it up. Only institutes in Mexico, China and Brazil said that sales would be subject to the production of an export licence.

4

IRAQ'S SECRET BIOLOGICAL WEAPONS

"The subjects we interviewed were, on the whole, fairly arrogant ... They were confident that we would not be able to find out anything. Later, some officials became scared and nervous... Some were even threatened by Iraqi officials in our presence. One gave a story that technically and scientifically could not have been true. He asked for a break, then gave a new story which was equally illogical. He produced a third story, a couple of days later. This chap told us later he was so nervous at this time that he could not keep any food down. The ones who were scared had good reason to be so."—*Rod Barton, UNSCOM inspector.*

On 11 December, 1998, US President Clinton and UK Prime Minister Tony Blair agreed to bomb Iraq. The United Nations was reporting that Iraqi President Saddam Hussein was continuing to break the agreement he had signed in 1991 at the end of the Gulf War, under which he promised to reveal the extent of his biological weapons.

For seven years the United Nations had been trying, with some success, to outwit the Iraqis' efforts to duck this obligation. The UN report of yet more Iraqi non-compliance helped bring US frustration—possibly stoked by Clinton's domestic political difficulties—to the boil. On 16 December the attack began. For four nights, cruise missiles and other bombs sought out Iraq's weapons installations, air defence facilities, state security apparatus and the Republican Guard—the elite force close to Saddam. One of the targets of British bombs was an airbase at Talil in south-east Iraq, which the British said housed unmanned aircraft which could be fitted with aerosols to spray biological weapons.[1] It now seems highly unlikely that Iraq will allow any more inspectors from the United Nations Special Commission on Iraq (UNSCOM) to continue their efforts to uncover any remaining preparations for biological war.

UNSCOM

UNSCOM was set up by the United Nations in 1991, following Iraq's invasion of Kuwait and the subsequent Gulf War. The cease-fire arrangements at the end of the war tried to reduce the threat posed by Iraq's weapons. The UN Security Council demanded that the defeated state should not acquire or develop nuclear weapons, and it made the International Atomic Energy Agency responsible for preventing this. It also laid down that Iraq must accept the "destruction, removal or rendering harmless"[2] of missiles with a range of more than 150 kilometers, and all chemical and biological weapons. This disarmament should be supervised by an international body which would have unrestricted access to Iraqi facilities. Thus UNSCOM was born.

The idea was that Iraq would make a clean breast of its chemical, biological and missile capabilities to the UN. As far as its biological weapons programme was concerned, it would give details of the locations in which it had carried out research, development, support and manufacturing. It would specify the types of agents it had worked on and the amount it had stockpiled. Working on the basis of Iraq's declarations, UNSCOM would inspect the facilities to check that its activities tallied with its declarations.

Hardly surprisingly, Iraq was less than enthusiastic about the plan. For the first two years of UNSCOM's life it refused, in effect, to cooperate. The task facing the inspectors was daunting. They had no evidence that Iraq had developed biological weapons. There had been rumours, but no proof. And the nature of biological weapons made their job all the harder.

It is relatively easy to detect whether a state is developing and deploying nuclear weapons. The production of the fissile materials for a militarily significant number of nuclear weapons, for example, requires quite large plants which are extremely easy to detect by, say, reconnaissance satellites. But biological weapons are different. The bacteria and viruses they depend on are produced in exactly the same way as those used for legitimate health-care: for vaccines and antibiotics. Micro-organisms for biological weapons are produced in the same equipment that can be found in pharmaceutical companies, university biological laboratories, breweries, distilleries, dairies, diagnostic laboratories and vaccine-producing facilities. Once, it was hard to produce micro-organisms on a large scale. These days, modern biotechnology makes it easy; and the know-how as well as the equipment is commonplace. The equipment that can be used for both military and civilian purposes is called "dual-use"; and it presents a problem that lies at the heart of controlling the development of biological weapons. It presented the UNSCOM team with a huge complication. They were charged with monitoring Iraq's dual-use equipment to make sure it was only being used for innocent purposes. But they needed Iraq to tell them about its past clandestine programmes and its current legitimate ones, to form a baseline from which ongoing activities could be monitored. And Iraq refused. After a lot of pressure, however, it did admit in May 1992 to having had a very small, defensive biological research programme—but no weapons.

On paper, the inspectors' powers were formidable. They could inspect anything—site, activity, material—unannounced, as often as they liked; they could fly over whatever they wanted for surveillance purposes, using their own aircraft. They could install sensors and video recorders in sensitive locations; they could take pictures; they could collect information from other countries about what pieces of dual-use equipment they had exported to Iraq. But it was not until January 1994 that Iraq gave UNSCOM enough information for them to organise meaningful inspections for biological capabilities. The first such inspection, which was to establish the baseline against which others would be judged, was carried out in April that year.

WORKING WITH UNSCOM

Rod Barton, then of the Australian Department of Defence, was sent to Baghdad in September 1994 to be part of an UNSCOM team. It was not his first taste of Iraqi methods: he had already tried, again with UNSCOM, to uncover the full extent of Iraq's chemical weapons programme. When he joined the effort to discover whether Iraq had developed biological weapons as well, he was in for an exciting time.

As Barton recalls in the journal *Pacific Research,* things did not look hopeful. "The Iraqi government persistently denied that it had developed biological weapons, saying that UNSCOM had had free rein for three years to go anywhere, look anywhere, and had found nothing."[3] He continues:

"Iraq had admitted to having the research programme. They said this facility was at Salman Pak, which had been heavily bombed during the war, so there was not much left of it. Iraq also had another facility , at al-Hakam, that was not known to coalition governments before the Gulf War, and therefore was not bombed. The inspectors were told that it was a biological facility for producing yeast for animal feed. Inspection teams had visited it frequently, as it seemed an odd place which didn't make technical sense, but were not able to gather any hard evidence that it was anything other than what the Iraqis claimed.

"We decided to ask supporting countries for information about imports into Iraq. The lists we got were quite comprehensive, but most items were dual-use in nature, so it was not easy to sort out what was legitimate from what was not.

"In addition, the team decided to interview Iraqi officials who had been involved. All ten people from Salman Pak that we asked to interview turned out to be now at al-Hakam, far from driving taxis or doing whatever jobs they could find, as Iraqi officials had told us. This gave us a link between Salman Pak and al-Hakam. It was clear to the inspection team as they interviewed the ten that all had been coached, and our suspicions were raised. Every single one said they knew nothing about anyone else, not even about people who had worked in the room next door, which the inspectors did not find believable. But we were not able to get much more out of them.

"Two wild cards proved very useful—the names of individuals who had signed import orders. These, it turned out, were not scientists but clerks. One had been working for the Technical Scientific Materials Import Division (TSMID), an import organisation apparently connected with the Ministry of Trade. A breakthrough came when one of the clerks confessed that TSMID had been importing *only* for Salman Pak, nowhere else. This turned out to be vital information.

"The subjects interviewed in November 1994 were, on the whole, fairly arrogant and dismissive of the UNSCOM inspectors, as were Iraqi officials. They were confident that we would not be able to find out anything. Later, some officials became scared and nervous in the presence of the UNSCOM inspectors, and evinced signs of feeling threatened. Some were even threatened by Iraqi officials in our presence. One gave a story that technically and scientifically could not have been true. He asked for a break, then gave a new story which was equally illogical. He produced a third story, a couple of days later. This chap told us later he was so nervous at this time that he could not keep any food down. The ones who were scared had good reason to be so.

"We had one other breakthrough, from the information on imports provided by other governments. In 1988 TSMID had imported many tons of bacterial growth media—stuff to grow bacteria on (consisting of casein from milk, with other proteins and glucose). It was legitimate to grow bacteria for research, but you would need only, maybe, one kilogram for research. If Salman Pak was using so much, then it could not be just for defence research. It must have been for something more aggressive."

The Iraqis denied that they had imported large quantities of growth media, but the UNSCOM inspectors quoted letter-of-credit numbers as proof that they had. The Iraqis then said the media had been used for the Ministry of Health for hospital use. The inspectors were suspicious. "We checked with hospitals in different places," recalls Rod Barton, "and found out, for example, that one big New York hospital might use a few kilos a year. We found that one whole country in the Middle East had used only a few tons over five years. By this stage we had discovered that TSMID had imported over 40 tons of growth media. The Iraqis told us the Minister of Health had made a mistake and ordered much more than was needed. But the types of growth media were wrong, the quantities were wrong, and they were in the wrong containers for hospital use. Some was in 25 kg containers, and some in 100 kg drums. This was not believable as quantities for hospital use, where you would need only a few grams at a time. Because, like milk powder, it cakes if you take the lid off and don't use it quickly, and you would expect it to be in small jars."

The inspectors tried to track the media down through documentation. Iraq produced 22 documents—receipts, transfer documents and store inventory cards—which forensic analysis showed to be recently created. The originals, said the Iraqis, had been the only documents in a filing cabinet which had been destroyed in a fire. Comments Barton: "The story was patently absurd. We asked for a report from the fire brigade. Was the office burnt down? No, it was just the filing cabinet. What was the cabinet made of? Steel. Was anything else burnt? No, there was nothing else in the cabinet. We asked for originals of the transfer receipts, and were told these had fallen off the back of a truck during a transfer from one store to another. With the third set of documents, the store inventory cards, the storeman got to the point where it was obvious his stories were absurd and there was no believable explanation for how the originals had been destroyed. We interviewed this poor storeman for hours."

The inspectors' interviews were taking place against a background of UN sanctions against Iraq. These had been imposed in August 1990, after Iraq had invaded Kuwait, in an attempt to force its withdrawal. When UNSCOM was set up, in 1991, the UN declared that sanctions would not be lifted until Iraq had cooperated fully with its activities. By 1994, the sanctions had impoverished the country and were causing appalling hardship to its people: widespread poverty and hunger, and an almost total breakdown of medical services. In April, 1995, the team reported to the UN Security Council that although they had no proof that Iraq had biological weapons, they did have circumstantial evidence. Back in Iraq, in May and June, officials refused to speak to the inspectors. "They said we were responsible for sanctions not being lifted; we were responsible for children dying," remembers Rod Barton. "On one occasion they actually brought dying children to our hotel, and there was a demonstration by doctors and nurses against UNSCOM."

In July, the Iraqis changed their story yet again. "In a half-hour presentation, the head of the defensive research programme admitted that Iraq had developed a biological weapons programme, that it had started at Salman Pak and then gone to al-Hakam. The plants produced bacterial agents for anthrax and botulinum toxin, about half a million litres. This would account for about 17 tons of the missing growth media. We asked if weapons had been made, and got the answer, 'There were no weapons, we just produced and stored agent.'"

On 7 August 1995, Saddam Hussein's son-in-law, General Hussein Kamel Hassan Majeed, fled Baghdad for asylum in Jordan. He had been in charge of all of Iraq's nuclear, chemical and biological weapons programmes. The Iraqis firstly tried to persuade him to return, and when this failed they apparently tried to assassinate him. This also failed; so the Iraqis admitted, finally, that they had made and deployed biological weapons. "In the circumstance of potential disclosures by the most well-informed defector possible, the Iraqi government decided to pre-empt that eventuality by making them itself," writes Milton Leitenberg, of the Center for International and Security Studies at the University of Maryland.[4] "They admitted," recounts Rod Barton, "that Iraq had made gas gangrene, anthrax, botulinum toxin, viral and fungal agents (including aflatoxin), agents against crops (such as wheat smut), and ricin (a deadly poison made from castor beans). These agents had been made not only at al-Hakam but at other plants. There was a vast organisation, which employed many people.

"UNSCOM was surprised—we hadn't expected the biological weapons programme to have been so big."

One of the more bizarre events of the saga occurred in connection with these admissions. When General Hussein Kamel Hassan Majeed fled from Baghdad, the Iraqi government informed UNSCOM's Chairman, Ambassador Rolf Ekeus, that it had more information to add to its previous disclosures. It was to Ekeus that the Iraqis made their admissions. Ekeus complained that he had not been given any documentation to support the new disclosures. As he was about to go to the airport to leave the country, he was contacted by an Iraqi General who asked him to call in to a farm on the way to the airport. It was General Hussein Kamel Hassan Majeed's farm, and in a locked chicken house there, Ekeus found 150 "metal and wooden boxes which were packed with documentation, together with microfiches, computer diskettes, videotapes, photographs and prohibited hardware components."[5] In all, there were well over half a million pages of documentation, much of it about UNSCOM's areas of interest. The Iraqis subsequently admitted that, in the summer of 1991, the directors of the sites involved in the biological weapons programme had been ordered to pack up important documents quickly, and hand them over to the security organizations.

The documents recovered from the chicken coop were an important breakthrough for UNSCOM, but by no means do they provide a complete record of Iraq's biological weapons programme. Much is still missing.

Ambassador Ekeus is not convinced that Iraq divulged the full scope of its biological weapons programme. He suggests that Iraq wanted the UN to lift its sanctions without ever having to reveal its biological programme. "They kept biology as the prize," he concludes. "The suspicion that Iraq is still concealing a great deal cannot be dismissed lightly. If you had seen the officers, who had denied everything until recently, admit the existence of biological weapons without blushing, without feeling any remorse, you would understand why many in the United Nations still have doubts about Iraq's credibility."[6]

Had Iraq's weapons been used, says Ekeus, they "would have killed millions of people. What shocks me in retrospect is the realisation that the world was facing an enormous catastrophe, of which we did not even have a clue."

How much do we currently know about Iraq's BW programme? The information it has released leads the UNSCOM inspectors to draw the following (probably incomplete) picture:

The programme began in 1975, achieved little and was closed down in 1978. It was re-started in 1985, at the Muthanna State Establishment, Iraq's main facility for chemical weapons research and development. In April 1986, bacterial strains were imported to Muthanna (it has been reported that the anthrax culture was bought by mail order from the US, and sent by overnight mail),[7] and work began on anthrax and botulinum toxin. In May 1987, the programme moved to Al Salman, where the agents were tested on sheep, donkeys, monkeys and dogs. A former biotechnology plant at Taji was also taken over for weapons production in mid-1987. At the end of that year it was decided to step the programme up, and in 1988 a new weapons production facility was built and equipped at Al Hakam. It included space for studies of genetic engineering and work on viruses. Meanwhile, at Al Salman, work began on the agent that produces gas gangrene (Clostridium perfringens) and aflatoxin (a poison which induces liver cancer several years after exposure. Researchers at the Stockholm International Peace Research have speculated that it may have been intended as a genocidal weapon against the Kurds. By the time symptoms appeared, there would be no way of proving that they had been the victims of biological warfare. Aflatoxin may also have been intended as an immune suppressant, to make other agents act more effectively).[8] Later research was also done on toxins which produce nausea, vomiting, diarrhoea and skin irritation; on ricin, a lethal toxin; on haemorrhagic conjunctivitis virus which causes acute pain and temporary blindness; and on rotavirus which causes diarrhea. UNSCOM uncovered circumstantial evidence that some of these agents may have been tested on human subjects.

The programme was not confined to agents that would harm people. It also worked on camel pox which causes fever and skin rash in camels, and black stem rust of wheat which causes severe crop losses.

The programme was drastically intensified after Iraq invaded Kuwait in August, 1990. By December of that year, the Iraqis had produced 166 R400 aerial bombs filled with biological agents: 100 with botulinum, 50 with anthrax and 16 with aflatoxin. They had also made a special BW warhead for the Al Husayn ("Super-Scud") missile: 25 of them; 13 filled with botulinum toxin, 10 with anthrax and 2 with aflatoxin. Just before the beginning of the Gulf War, in January 1991, these weapons were dispersed to four locations throughout the country where they remained during the war. During the war, Iraq pre-delegated authority to launch the weapons in the event that Baghdad suffered nuclear attack. Comments UNSCOM: "This pre-delegation does not exclude the alternative use of such a capability and therefore does not constitute proof of only intentions concerning second use."[9]

Professor Paul Rogers, of the University of Bradford's Department of Peace Studies, comments: "If BW or chemical warfare agents had been used in the conflict on a substantial scale, and if the attack had been successfully undertaken against civilian targets such as Riyadh, Dhahran or Tel Aviv, casualties would have been broadly similar to those caused by nuclear weapons. A recent US Department of Defense simulation exercise of a future Gulf crisis ended with a BW attack on Dhahran killing one million people, followed by a US nuclear retaliation against Baghdad."[10]

Iraq claims that it destroyed most of its BW facilities after the war, but its reports of this destruction have been inconsistent and it has not offered any proof to back them up. Meanwhile, UNSCOM is physically demolishing the Al Hakam site. Explains Rod Barton: "Nothing will remain of the facility. The equipment will be crushed and the scrap buried in pits back-filled with concrete. The building will be blown up and the foundations removed. Even the power lines will be pulled down and the access roads bulldozed. Essentially the site will be returned to the desert, so that nothing will remain that can be used for biological weapons purposes again. Perhaps then this chapter on Iraq will be closed."

Others are less hopeful. Microbiologist Raymond Zilinskas, of the University of Maryland Biotechnology Institute, was also seconded to UNSCOM and took part in two inspections in Iraq in 1994. He draws different conclusions from his experience: ". . . as far as is known, none of the persons who staffed Iraq's former BW program were harmed or killed during Desert Storm. We may assume that all of them would be available to staff a resurgent BW program, should the Iraqi leadership so decide. Similarly, the same Iraqi leadership that decided to acquire biological weapons—and therefore launched Iraq's former BW program—remains intact and in charge."[11] Thus the political will and the intellectual knowledge remain in place. A briefing paper written for UK Members of Parliament also points out: "stores of freeze-dried organisms could be easy to keep and hide, allowing a BW programme to be swiftly re-instated . . . [T]he concerns are that production of militarily significant quantities could resume in as little as 6 months."[12]

Iraq's clandestine efforts to develop biological weapons are by no means the first. Since the 1920s, the Western allies, Japan and the former Soviet Union have all done extensive work on agents and weapons. The next two chapters describe these programmes, and how weapons were both prepared for use and actually used.

WITH A LITTLE HELP

There seems little doubt that the Americans helped the Iraqis develop biological weapons. American organisations supplied microbes to the Iraqis for 20 years—during the 1970s and 1980s.

The American Type Culture Collection (ATCC) is a non-profit firm based in Rockville, Maryland. It has the nation's leading collection of cultured diseases, and acts as a library of about 1,000 microbes for institutions all over the world. It sells approximately 130,000 cultures annually and ships orders to 60 nations—including Iraq. ATCC supplied 17 shipments to Iraq between 1986 and 1991. Director Robert Stevenson refused to say exactly what he had sold to the Iraqis, but tularemia is known to have been among the samples.

The shipments, which contained attenuated strains of various toxins and bacteria, went to Iraq's Atomic Energy Commission which is believed to have procured components for biological weapons. Although the exports were not vetted by Pentagon or intelligence analysts, they were approved by the Department of Commerce. Robert Stevenson is also the head of the Commerce Department's advisory committee on biological exports.

Although Stevenson admitted that he did not really know who in Iraq was using his microbes, he insisted that there was nothing to worry about. He claimed that the materials he sent would be of no use for biological warfare—although he conceded that ATCC cultures would be "useful" in a biological warfare program as "reference points" to determine if the deadly strain was the real thing. The Commerce committee took him at his word.

ATCC was not the only organisation to export micro-organisms to Iraq. In April 1990, NBC television reported that during the 1980's the US Public Health Service's Centers for Disease Control shipped deadly viruses via Express Mail to researchers in Iraq, South Africa, Cuba, the Soviet Union and China—all nations suspected of biological warfare research—ostensibly for public health reasons. According to NBC producer Robert Windrum and reporter Eric Nadler, "the virus requested by, and supplied to, an Iraqi researcher in Basra was an Israeli strain of West Nile encephalitis. The virus had been the subject of a long-term vaccine research project in Israel supported by the US Army because of its potential as a bio-warfare agent. The same virus was a cause of concern inside the Israeli defense forces medical corps due to outbreaks in Negev desert posts in the early 1980s. When NBC asked the CDC to provide documentation of these exports under the Freedom of Information Act, the center said it had no records, since such transfers are handled 'informally.' "

Remarkably, CDC staffers expressed no fear that the exported agents (all Biohazard level 3 and 4 materials—the deadliest classification) would be used for germ warfare, 'because we know these people,' as CDC spokesperson Gayle Lloyd breezily put it. She called any biological war scenario 'far-fetched'."

The NBC report put an end to CDC biological shipments to Iraq. (Source: Eric Nadler and Robert Windrem, *San Diego Union-Tribune*, 26 January 1991, pB-11.)

UK AID

The UK also helped Saddam Hussein develop his biological arsenal—by training one of the Iraqi scientists in charge of the germ warfare unit.[13]

Dr Taha Rihab was awarded her PhD in plant pathology at the University of East Anglia in 1984. She had come to the University from one in Iraq. Her PhD work was on a disease of tobacco plants. "She really was an outstanding student," recalls one of her lecturers, Dr John Turner. "Hard working, very dedicated and absolutely charming. Not in my wildest dreams would I have thought of her in [weapons] work."

The revelation gives an ironic twist to the fears of scientists afraid that their work could be used for aggressive purposes. It shows how easy it is for people educated in good faith to use their skills for offensive ends, and how difficult it would be to try to stop the spread of knowledge needed for biological warfare.

GULF WAR SYNDROME

Major Hillary Jones came back to the UK from the Gulf with a flu-like illness that she could not shake off. She had a persistent cough and developed chronic fatigue syndrome, whose exact cause is unknown but which many believe to be associated with prolonged exposure to viruses. Major Jones was forced to give up her work as a nurse lecturer. She is one of the ex-service personnel claiming her health was damaged because of service in the Gulf, and suffering what has come to be called Gulf War Syndrome.

Other ex-Gulf personnel have suffered from skin rashes, headaches, nausea, musculoskeletal problems and depression. There have been claims that children born to men who served in the Gulf have shown a higher-than-normal incidence of birth defects. More than 1,000 veterans have issued the Ministry of Defence with writs claiming compensation for the syndrome and its effects.

After years of denial that there was any problem, the British government finally agreed in December 1996 to set up two epidemiological studies to see whether Gulf War veterans have suffered as a result of their service. One study, based at the University of Manchester, will compare the health of 3,000 veterans with 3,000 matched service personnel who did not go to the Gulf. The other one, at the London School of Hygiene and Tropical Medicine, will compare the reproductive health of Gulf and non-Gulf personnel, as well as the health of their children. Both studies began in January 1997 and will take three years to complete. However, the MoD has failed to keep proper records about which personnel were given which drugs. These failings may scupper the reliability of the studies. They also point to the need for better administration, and raise yet again the question of whether secrecy does not inevitably lead to carelessness, sloppiness and reluctance to admit mistakes.

As well as the usual jabs against hepatitis B, typhoid, tetanus, polio, yellow fever, and meningitis, service personnel sent to the Gulf were vaccinated with a pertussis/anthrax combination, a US-made vaccine against bubonic plague, and a botulism vaccine. Since the war, the UK government has admitted that one of these was unlicensed.[14] *Chemistry in Britain* reports that the National Institute of Biological Standards and Control (NIBSC) "had tested two of the vaccines on animals and had warned the Ministry of Defence (MoD) in a fax in December 1990 that they were unsafe when used in combination. The MoD logged receipt of the fax, but then lost it and no action was taken. In the fax, NIBSC had warned against administering pertussis (whooping cough) vaccine to accelerate the onset of immunity conferred by anthrax vaccine. In laboratory tests, animals given this combination had become ill. Pertussis is not licensed for use on adults in the UK."

The troops also received tablets to protect against nerve gas poisoning which were not licensed until two years after the war.

The fact that a medication is unlicensed does not necessarily mean that it is dangerous. But the effects of using so many vaccines in combination are also unknown. As Dr Graham Pearson, formerly director of the chemical and biological defence establishment at Porton Down, told a House of Commons Defence Committee, most of the research "is concerned with the effectiveness of a specific vaccine, and is not particularly looking into how that will be administered in war [or the] particular circumstance that requires them all to be done together two days before you deploy."

Another suggested culprit for the health problems is nerve gas which blew over Allied troops after they blew up an ammunition depot where it was stored.

Another cause of the troops' illnesses may be organophosphate pesticides, used to prevent troops contracting flyborne diseases. The Ministry of Defence misled Parliament about the amount used, dramatically underestimating it for more than two years.

The American government also faces problems in trying to investigate their personnel's exposure to hazards, as their records are also incomplete. After repeated refusals to allow access to a crucial chemical warfare log kept for American commanders, the Pentagon admitted that more than three-quarters of it is missing.

GULF VETERANS ILL BUT NOT WITH GULF WAR SYNDROME

In January 1999, a US-funded study of UK Gulf War veterans found that they are more likely than those who served in Bosnia to develop symptoms of what has been dubbed Gulf War Syndrome. "Our study provides the first clear proof that going to the Gulf has affected the health of our soldiers," said one of the project's leaders, Professor Simon Wessley from the School of Medicine, King's College London.

The study also found that the Syndrome itself is not peculiar to Gulf War veterans. Bosnian veterans also reported headache, fatigue, chest pain, poor concentration, asthma, arthritis, dematitis, although less than Gulf veterans. Bosnian veterans also reported chronic fatigue and post-traumatic stress, although only half as often as Gulf veterans. The only factor which caused health effects in the Gulf veterans and not in the Bosnian veterans was the multiple vaccinations.

The study therefore suggests that there is no such thing as "Gulf War Syndrome"—although this does not mean that sick veterans do not have a genuine illness. "It is probably impossible to prevent all ill health after active combat duties, but we must do a better job in preparation, support and subsequent monitoring," said the study's other leader, Professor Anthony David of King's College London.

5

BROTHERS IN ARMS: UK, US AND CANADIAN PROGRAMS

Biological weapons research in the UK, United States and Canada was intimately connected until well after the Second World War. The British were the first to start thinking about it. They were alarmed in 1943 by reports that the Germans were conducting their own BW research,[1] and began to discuss the possibilities. Colonel Sir Maurice Hankey, Secretary of the Committee for Imperial Defence (CID), was the moving force behind the initiative; and on 12 February 1934 he told a meeting of the Chiefs of Staff that he "was wondering whether it might not be right to consider the possibilities and potentialities of this form of war."[2] Hankey was a humorless bureaucrat who was prepared to become deeply involved in promoting research into various forms of biological warfare even though he was convinced "that we should under no circumstances initiate these forms of frightfulness"—adding "although the possibility of retaliation, e.g., under pressure of public demand, could not be excluded."[3] In November 1936 he chaired a new subcommittee of the CID, which was to "report on the practicability of the introduction of biological warfare and to make recommendations as to the countermeasures which should be taken to deal with such an eventuality."[4]

Meanwhile, the Canadians' interest was awakening. John Bryden, whose book *Deadly Allies* traces the development of the Canadian biological and chemical programmes (see note 3), speculates that they may have been stirred into action in 1936 by fascist Italy's use of mustard gas on civilians in its war in Abyssinia. This was chemical, rather than biological, warfare, but it would have had special resonance for the president of Canada's National Research Council, General Andrew McNaughton, who had seen gas attacks when he fought at Ypres in the First World War. In September 1937, he had a conversation with Sir Frederick Banting, the Nobel Prize-winning co-discoverer of insulin, in which they discussed the possibilities of BW. Banting had been a medical officer in the War, and was no stranger to the effects of gas. He pointed out that the development of the aeroplane had opened up new opportunities for spreading infection over open reservoirs. They started lobbying for Canada to begin its own research. On November 1939, Banting and a colleague were terrified by a wartime crossing of the Atlantic, on a visit designed to see what research the British were doing. Afraid of being sunk by submarines, Banting promised to tow his colleague, who could not swim, if they found themselves in the water. Their planned defence against their fear and the elements was to keep talking to each other.[5] The two men arrived safely, and went on to Porton Down.

Porton Down was the official site of the UK's research into chemical and biological warfare. These days its official remit restricts its energies to defensive research. Established in 1916, it covers 7,000 acres on the southern edge of Salisbury Plain, and boasts "more species of butterflies than anywhere else in the United Kingdom"[6] on its chalk grasslands. At the time of Banting's visit the British, in spite of the aggressive-sounding remit of the official deliberations, felt no urgency about the sort of BW research he proposed. Their main worry reflected the concept, prevalent up to the War, that disease would most likely be caused by conventional bombing and its disruption of public health infrastuctures.[7] It may have been for this reason that the British had not considered much more than how vaccines could be made available to the population. Their sub-committee had metamorphosed into the Emergency Public Health Laboratory Service (EPHLS): a title chosen especially by one of its members, Sir Edward Mellanby, as not being "disturbing to the public mind." Although war had been declared, Mellanby, who was then Secretary of the Medical Research Council, did not think the Germans would use biological weapons—except possibly foot and mouth disease against cattle—and told Banting that the Council would never do research in the area. Banting was so annoyed by the laid-back attitude of the British that, back home again, he described Hankey in his diary as "a superb example of the servile, all-important complacent superior ass that runs the British government."[8]

In 1940 Banting applied for and was granted $25,000 for Canada's first officially-funded BW research. Based at the University of Toronto's Connaught Laboratories, it aimed to mix infectious bacteria with sawdust and deliver them from an aeroplane. The project did get as far as a trial of dispersing different grades of sawdust from a plane over Balsam Lake, north-east of Toronto—chosen because one of the scientists involved had a cottage there. Banting was very enthusiastic about the experiment, but John Bryden sums it up by saying that it "proved little more than that gravity works."[9] Nevertheless, in the months that followed, the government gave the go-ahead for a group to be created to produce bacteria, and Banting had a series of consultations with Canadian scientists about how best to develop a capacity for biological warfare. Dr Donald Fraser at the Connaught experimented with typhoid but found it unsatisfactory, as although it could be dried on sawdust, it lost its virulence when reactivated. Fraser evidently found the agent which causes salmonella poisoning to be a better bet, and Bryden describes his work as appearing to be "the first-ever attempt among English-speaking nations to cultivate a bacterial agent specifically for use against humans."[10] At this stage, the Canadians were working on BW more aggressively than the British.

As far as the British effort went, Banting had been more persuasive than he realised. In 1940, Hankey agitated for the UK to begin practical BW tests. The official history of Porton Down cites "communications with Sir Frederick Banting of Canada" as one of the reasons for the UK's renewed vigour.[11] Banting himself would have found that deeply satisfying, had he ever found out. In February 1941, wanting to see what progress the UK was making, he hitched a lift on a bomber flying to England. It crashed in Newfoundland and he was killed.

Hankey's efforts resulted in a secret group being set up at Porton in October 1940 to discover whether BW was feasible and how the country could retaliate. Mellanby found this development disturbing to his own mind (see box) and left the work to others: specifically to another Medical Research Council scientist, the eminent bacteriologist Dr Paul Fildes. From then on, the British BW effort intensified. The British were to make extensive use of Canadian help, especially with space for testing. In 1941, the Canadians made nearly one thousand square miles of semi-arid grassland in Alberta available for agent trials.

THE BRITISH PROGRAMME

The half-timbered Old George Hotel in Salisbury's High Street is thought to have been built in about 1320. Its distinctive bow windows were added during the seventeenth century; and by 1941 its superior status was attested by its affiliation, not only with the Royal Automobile Club and the Automobile Association, but with the American Automobile Association as well. Boasting some central heating and gas fires in most bedrooms, it must have been a comfortable billet for Paul Fildes, who lived there during the years he spent at Porton. By all accounts, he was a singular man. In 1940 he was a confirmed bachelor of 58 with a quirky sense of humor; arrogant, determined, autocratic, "with a quiet, ruminative way of speaking that never varied, even in anger or when, as sometimes happened, he was being devastatingly rude. Those who got to know him had for him a lasting, if occasionally rueful, affection . . ."[12] He was also a firm believer in the need for research into biological warfare. By the end of 1940, he had determined the most effective way to wage it: to manufacture something like a bomb that would burst, spewing out an aerosol consisting of particles of just the right size to be taken up and held in the lung. The aerosol would contain bacteria. Anyone in the target area would inhale them in sufficient numbers to cause disease.

The two agents that interested Fildes most were anthrax bacteria and botulinum toxin. He and his small group—there were never more than about 45 of them—went on to expose laboratory animals to anthrax spores, and to determine how many spores they needed to inhale to kill them. They also did field tests to see what concentration of spores could be suspended in aerosol dispersed from bomblets and how far the resulting cloud would waft downwind. The Porton area was too small for them to use anthrax spores for these field tests—they could not risk killing the inhabitants of the surrounding villages—so they used a harmless sporing bacterium they isolated from hay at Porton, instead. This work occupied the group during 1941. And in December of that year, they asked Prime Minister Winston Churchill for permission to produce the West's first biological weapon.

OPERATION VEGETARIAN

Lord Hankey, who wrote the request to Churchill, decided that the only weapon that was technically feasible was one to kill cattle. It was a crude affair, and it was not meant to initiate biological warfare; but it would have provided an effective retaliation against Germany if the Germans had used BW against the British. Not that there was much reason, except mistrust, to think they would.[13] However, the Chiefs of Staff gave the go-ahead for the project, and production began at Porton in the autumn of 1942.

"Operation Vegetarian" took the form of cattle cakes filled with anthrax. The idea was to drop them from planes over German agricultural districts, so that the cattle would die and the food supply would be disrupted. The cakes were made from finely ground linseed meal by a Bond Street soap maker and perfumer. They had a hollow well in the centre which, once they were delivered to Porton, was filled with anthrax spores before being sealed. The official accounts of this episode suggest its quaintness; its unlikeliness as a weapon of war; the whole process, once established, "was essentially run by one technician . . . , 15 ladies from a Bristol soap factory who were employed at Porton during the war for ad hoc small production jobs, one laboratory assistant, two labourers and "one boy to assist."[14] Official government papers released in 1999, however, show that the scientists admitted they were "playing with fire" with "mere children working in the laboratory, unskilled girls working in the factory [and] untrained personnel as laboratory assistants." It was a large project. It is hard to see how, in view of it, the British representative could have told the 1969 United Nations General Assembly that ". . . as successive British governments have made very clear, we have never had any biological weapons . . ."[15] Porton produced five million cakes, which were ready for use by April 1943.

They were never used. The stockpile was destroyed soon after the War except for a few kept until 1972 as memorabilia, when they were also destroyed.

What effect would they have had if they had rained down over German agricultural land? Gradon Carter of Porton Down writes: "The cakes were not intended to target man through eating the meat of infected cattle: cooking would have been generally effective in sterilising contaminated meat. The weapon was anti-livestock . . ."[16] Yet people could have been affected. They would have handled contaminated animals and been liable to contract cutaneous anthrax (curable with antibiotics) through cuts in their skin. If they had eaten meat from a dying animal without cooking it properly, they would probably have died themselves from gastrointestinal anthrax. Cattle would not have been the only consumers: rabbits, hedgehogs etc. may well have gnawed at the cakes, exposing the spores and causing local contamination which would have lasted for decades.

Anthrax spores are amazingly hardy. During 1998, scientists at Porton Down revived anthrax organisms from samples which had been stored for sabotage by the Germans for 80 years (see Chapter 6). As we will see below, the anthrax experiments the British themselves conducted on the Scottish island of Gruinard left the land so polluted that it was not judged safe to occupy until an intensive clean-up operation 47 years later. Local contamination would therefore have been a serious matter. And the Swedish National Defence Research Establishment raises another concern: that of the local animal population harbouring the infection and repeatedly passing it on to the human population. Following an attack with any micro-organism that can be spread from animals to humans, it says, "the infectious agent would be difficult to fight . . . as sporadic epidemics would break out for a long period after the attack."[17] Anthrax is one such micro-organism.

Zimbabwe has seen how this works in practice. In 1978–80, during the last phase of the war which led to the founding of the state of Zimbabwe, there was a massive outbreak of anthrax which affected both humans and animals. The epidemic has been labelled biological warfare, waged by white Rhodesians against cattle of tribesmen assisting guerillas (see box). David Martin, Director of the Southern African Research and Documentation Centre in Harare, comments: "In 1978–80 Zimbabwe suffered an anthrax epizootic, a mass outbreak which affected humans and animals. From 1981 to 1985 inclusive a further 4,124 human cases have been reported compared to the 334 human cases reported from 1950 to 1978 inclusive. This means that the incidence of anthrax in Zimbabwe is now . . . constantly present . . . [T]he sins of previous generations remain to haunt us . . . anthrax and other potential weapons of biological warfare do not simply go away once the immediate war is over."[18]

It is hard to see how any British operation using the cattle cakes would have been as neat and tidy as the official line would have us believe. They were not used because the Germans did not use BW against the British. In fact, although the British did not know it at the time, it seems that the Germans did not start much BW research until mid-1943, by which time the cattle cakes had already been stockpiled.

Permission for Operation Vegetarian was sought at the end of 1941. The same month saw not only the entry of the US into the War, but a flurry of cooperation between it and Canada on plans for biological warfare.

THE US PROGRAM

Even before the US officially entered the War, the subject of biological warfare had been discussed. As early as September, 1940, the President of the Carnegie Institute—Dr Vannevar Bush—had suggested to Dr Weed of the medical committee of the US Council of National Defense that this committee was the proper place to consider "offensive and defensive measures in the field of human, animal and plant diseases."[19] At a meeting between Canadian bacteriologists Professor E G D Murray and Dr Guilford Reed, and US scientists, army and navy personnel in December 1941, in the Lord Baltimore Hotel, Baltimore, the scientists outlined the areas they were interested in pursuing. The list was long: botulinus toxin which could perhaps be used to poison water supplies; malaria, yellow fever, psittacosis, diphtheria, tetanus, salmonella and plague. The Americans had looked into the possibility of killing crop plants—potatoes, soybeans, rice, wheat—and had (like the Canadians) started experiments with toxic plant hormones. Against animals the group considered foot and mouth disease, pleuropneumonia, African horse sickness, glanders and anthrax. But it was rinderpest which was most worrying. It was seen as a real threat to North American cattle. It killed up to 80 percent of the herds it infected, and at the time there was not much defence against it. The meeting agreed that research to combat it should have priority. A month later, Murray offered the Americans the perfect place to carry out rinderpest experiments. It was Grosse Ile, a small island in the St Lawrence, near Quebec City.

Grosse Ile had been used as a quarantine station for immigrants to Canada in the nineteenth century. Many of them had been Irish; twelve thousand had died there, of cholera. When the Canadians and Americans inspected the island in July, 1942, they found the school house complete with desks, and the Catholic and Protestant churches still with hymn books in the pews. The island, only two miles long and one wide, had other buildings which could easily be adapted for the scientists' purposes. Here they worked with their germs. The vaccine against rinderpest was achieved in 1945, but long before then the scientists became side-tracked into the allies' greatest collaborative project of the War: to produce anthrax bombs. In this, the British were the prime movers.

GRUINARD

While the Canadians and Americans had been getting together, the British had been busy producing anthrax both for their cattle cakes and as the preferred option in an anti-personnel weapon. Not satisfied with dummy trials at Porton, they wanted to experiment with the real thing; and by the summer of 1942 they were ready. The site they chose was Gruinard Island, in Gruinard Bay on the west coast of Scotland. The trials proved that biological warfare worked, and left the island so contaminated that it was not pronounced fit for habitation by man or beast until 1990 (see below).

Commentators on these events have presented the Gruinard trials as dangerous lunacy, on the one hand, or an example of the sober efficiency of government, on the other. Contemporary government records released in 1999 show that the scientists involved recognised the dangers. They privately acknowledged that the hazards were "uncontrollable." What became clear was that Fildes and his team, having chosen anthrax partly because of the longevity of its virulence, had no idea, when they undertook the tests, how to clean up after them. In May 1943, Fildes told the Canadians and the Americans about the Gruinard trials and their results. Ten months later, Churchill, realising that the UK could not develop an anthrax bomb capability on its own, ordered half a million anthrax bombs "as a first instalment" from the Americans. Designed by the British, made by the Americans and tested by the Canadians, the so-called N-bomb project was meant to deliver cluster bombs containing 4-lb sub-munitions filled with anthrax spores. The three countries put their energies into an anthrax weapon that could be used against people.

US AND CANADIAN DEVELOPMENTS

Soon after making Grosse Ile available for rinderpest development, the Canadian bacteriologist Professor Murray was able to expand the work to be done there to include producing anthrax for the British. In fact, anthrax bombs were tested at Suffield, the huge Canadian testing ground in Alberta, before the end of the War. Grosse Ile did produce anthrax, but not in sufficient quantities to satisfy demand; and the Americans took over production in August, 1944.

The Americans set up their own BW programme at Camp (later Fort) Detrick in Maryland, in April 1943. The previous May, President Roosevelt had approved research along the lines discussed at the Baltimore meeting in December, 1941, into offensive and defensive measures in the categories of botulinus toxin and diseases of man, animals, plants and food supplies. Work began at Camp Detrick on the cloud chamber project, which studied how animals became infected through breathing in germs. At the time, the mechanics of infection by inhalation had not been studied; and the project showed that this route could be used to spread disease. This in turn led on to the practicalities of how this could be done: studies of aerosols and how they could be produced by munitions.

The American BW programme was the largest. By the end of the War it employed nearly 4,000 military personnel and civilians. As well as Camp Detrick, work was carried out at the Granite Peak Installation in Utah, which from 1944 was used for field studies of living pathogens. Agents were produced at the Vigo plant at Terre Haute, Indiana. By November 1944, the Americans had produced the agents causing brucellosis, psittacosis, tularemia and glanders—as well as five anti-crop agents which were actually chemicals rather than biological weapons.[20] But most work went into anthrax and botulism. By May, 1944, the programme could produce 50,000 bombs a month—up to a quarter of the million by the end of that year—which could be filled with anthrax once it was itself produced. The bombs were to be shipped to Britain in case they were needed for use. In fact, the weapon was not ready before the end of the War.

It was just as well. The British had drawn up contingency plans to use anthrax bombs in reprisal on six German cities: Berlin, Hamburg, Stuttgart, Frankfurt, Wilhelmshafen and Aachen. They estimated that "50 percent of the inhabitants who were exposed to the cloud of anthrax without respirators would be killed by inhalation, while many more might die through subsequent contamination of the skin . . . The terrain will be contaminated for years, and danger from skin infection should be great enough to enforce evacuation."[21] In a BBC television interview in 1981, the then Director of CDE Porton, Dr R G H Watson, said that if those German cities had been bombed, they would very probably still be uninhabitable because of contamination. And he knew: it was CDE which was responsible for monitoring contamination on Gruinard.[22]

As the War turned out, the Germans did not attack the British with biological weapons and the British did not retaliate with them. The fact that there was no biological warfare between these two countries, however, may have been more a matter of their state of preparedness than their unwillingness to use BW. Germany's V-bomb attacks on Britain in June 1944, enraged Churchill, who considered using both chemical and biological weapons in retaliation. He clearly stated his moral position on the question of using gas against Germany in a memorandum to his Chiefs of Staff: "It is absurd to consider morality on this topic when everybody used it in the last war without a word of complaint from the moralists or the Church. On the other hand, in the last war the bombing of open cities was regarded as forbidden. Now everybody does it as a matter of course. It is simply a question of fashion changing as she does between long and short skirts for women."[23] In July, 1944, the Chiefs of Staff asked their Joint Planning Staff to examine methods of warfare they had previously refrained from using against the Germans, either as a counter-offensive to German flying bombs or as a means of shortening the war. The JPS was told to consider "the possibilities of the use of biological warfare by us or by the enemy. It should take the form of a thorough and practical examination of the military factors involved and should ignore ethical and political considerations."[24] The JPS replied that anthrax was "the only Allied biological agent which could probably make a material change in the war situation before the end of 1945 . . . There seems to be little doubt that the use of Biological warfare would cause heavy casualties, panic and confusion in the areas affected. It might lead to a breakdown in administration with a consequent decisive influence on the outcome of the war."[25] The JPS went on to say, however, that the US production programme was behind schedule, and that "there is no likelihood of a sustained attack being possible much before the middle of 1945." By which time there was no military need for it.

These memoranda make sobering reading. With Churchill in aggressive mode and ethical considerations explicitly being ignored, the Chiefs of Staff recommended against anthrax—evidently because it was not available. Had it been, would their decision have been different? Robert Kupperman, senior advisor to the Washington Center for Strategic and International Studies, and David Smith, a scientist at Los Alamos (where the atomic bomb was developed), are unequivocal: ". . . had World War II not ended when it did, biological weapons would undoubtedly have been used."[26] Such judgements must be influenced by the way the Allies acted in similar situations. When, a year later, they saw another way of shortening the War, ethical considerations did not stop them dropping atomic bombs on Japan.

The "frightfulness" of biological warfare that Lord Hankey abhorred had, by the end of the War, been thoroughly prepared for.

Malcolm Dando, Professor of International Security at the University of Bradford, summarises Britain's BW programme by saying that it "confirms high-level interest, the allocation of large-scale resources, a perception of biological warfare as a real possibility, the perceived vulnerability of Britain to strategic attack and, finally, the production of offensive biological weapons."[27] These factors apply equally to Canada and the United States. In all three countries, work continued after the War.

AFTER THE WAR

The BW programmes of the UK, Canada and the US followed different courses after the War. The UK abandoned its offensive research in 1957; by 1970, Canada was denying its wartime activities; and the US developed a large offensive programme before halting it in 1969.

THE UK

The immediate post-War years saw an expansion of the UK's involvement. In spite of the prevailing austerity, the programme was housed in a new building at Porton—"remarkable indicator of the importance attached to BW," according to Porton Down historian Gradon Carter.[28] Between 1948 and 1955, Porton and the Royal Navy conducted a series of trials to collect data on "the factors affecting the survival of pathogenic micro-organisms in aerosol under realistic field conditions"[29] After the experience of contaminating Gruinard, these trials were done at sea. Some took place in Scottish waters, others off the Bahamas. Pathogens thought to include anthrax, brucellosis and tularemia were released from munitions or sprayed over animals in rubber dinghies.[30] Carter says that by the end of the '50's, "the UK had a considerable knowledge of how putative BW agents behaved in the field"[31]—which presumably means the trials were successful. They seem to have had some hiccups, however: according to Bryden, "the British got into such trouble with one of these experiments that an expert from Suffield had to be sent down to help them out."[32] Other trials were conducted in the UK with simulants, to see how vulnerable the country would be to attack[33] (see box). The conclusion: no significant defence was possible.

Official documents show that the British policy was to concentrate on defence against BW. But this meant trials to provide the information they needed to understand the problems an effective defence would have to overcome.[34] Carter tells us that "the late 1950s saw a secret political decision to abandon all aims for a UK offensive capability and to restrict research to defensive needs."[35] Since then, defensive work has continued. We will return to the nature of Porton's current defensive work in Chapter 6.

CANADA

Little is known about Canadian post-War BW activities, but Canada signed the 1972 Biological Weapons Convention, which forbids the development, production, stockpiling or acquisition of BW, in April, 1972.

In 1946, Professor Reed drew up a list of all the BW projects Canada had done during and since the War. Altogether there were 36; nine of which were completed and 20 ongoing.[36] Clearly, Canada was still very interested in BW. The same year saw a US-Canadian conference at Suffield at which Dr Solandt, the new head of the Canadian Defence Research Board, hailed a new era of co-operation on chemical and biological weapons between the US, Canada and the UK. In 1970, however, the Canadian government told the United Nations that "Canada never has had and does not now possess any biological weapons (or toxins)..."[37] Bryden points out that this is hard to reconcile with the facts. Grosse Ile was still producing anthrax in 1944, and there is no official record of it ever being destroyed. "It was undoubtedly stored at Suffield," he says, "which had the facility to load it into bombs."[38] The Canadians had also taken delivery of more than a ton of botulinus toxin from the Americans in 1946.

THE US

"Work in this field, born of the necessity of war, cannot be ignored in times of peace..." Thus wrote George Merck, War-time leader of the War Research Service BW programme, to Secretary of War Henry Stimson, in 1946.[39] His view has prevailed: with several ups and downs, the US has, since the War, developed the largest and most sophisticated BW capability known to be possessed by any nation.

From 1943 until 1956, official policy declared that the country would not initiate BW, but use biological weapons only in retaliation. This policy came under increasing strain during the 1950s when, in the face of the Cold War and fear of the Soviet Union, several reviews urged an expansion of the BW programme. In 1956 the no-first-use policy was secretly revoked (although the change was not publicly admitted until 1977), and a huge expansion began. According to Susan Wright, an historian of science at the University of Michigan, support for the chemical and biological programmes rose by 2,000 percent in real terms between the early 1950's and 1969.[40] Over 300 universities, research institutes and corporations carried out research for the biological programme. Veteran investigative journalist Seymour Hersh relates that experiments on human subjects were authorised after 1955 and were carried out "particularly on Seventh Day Adventists serving noncombat Army duties as conscientious objectors [who] were exposed to airborne tularemia."[41] Hersh estimates that, at the beginning of the 1960's Fort Detrick could have been using up to 60,000 experimental animals—mice, rats, guinea pigs, monkeys—*every month* for BW experiments. By the end of the 1960s, the US military had weaponised and stockpiled three lethal agents (for anthrax, tularemia and botulin poisoning) and four incapacitating agents (for brucellosis, Q-fever, Venezuelan equine encephalitis and Staphyloccocal enterotoxin B poisoning).[42] It had studied more agents as well: those causing Rift Valley fever, Chikungunya disease, yellow fever, rabbit fever, psittacosis, Rocky Mountain spotted fever, and plague.[43] Neither had it overlooked plant pathogens. It stockpiled, but not weaponised, rice blast, wheat stem rust and rye stem rust. All were destroyed between 1971 and 1973.[44]

TESTS ON CIVILIANS

Edwin Nevin was a retired pipe-fitter who went into hospital in San Francisco in October, 1950 for a simple hernia operation. On 1 November he died of pneumonia, and blood and urine samples showed infection with *Serratia marcescens* bacteria. Doctors at the hospital were puzzled, because his case was one of eleven similar ones around the same time. Illness from *Serratia* had never before been recorded at the hospital. It was such a rare outbreak that they wrote it up for the *Archives of Internal Medicine* the following year. The article went unnoticed until 1976, when details of tests carried out by the Pentagon twenty-six years before began to appear. The Nevin family sat up and took notice.

Between 20 and 26 September, 1950, two US Navy minesweepers steamed up and down outside the Golden Gate Bridge, San Francisco, releasing clouds of *Serratia marcescens* and *Bacillus globigii*, both thought to be harmless, to see how they would disperse over the city. The Pentagon was worried that a Soviet submarine might release dangerous pathogens and disappear again before anyone became ill, and it wanted to see whether such an attack were feasible. The scientists traced the bacteria as they settled on the city, and concluded that practically everyone had inhaled 5000 particles.[45] The Pentagon had its answer.

The Nevin family sued the government for damages, arguing that Edward Nevin had died as a result of the BW test. The government maintained that the timings of the test and the outbreak at the hospital were coincidental. The government won.

There were six tests at San Francisco alone. Between 1949 and 1969, the Pentagon carried out 239 open air tests over populated areas including San Francisco, Minneapolis, Key West, St. Louis and Panama City. The army maintained that the bacteria were safe, and would simply simulate the behaviour of pathogens. This has been challenged by Leonard Cole, who teaches science and public policy at Rutgers University. He maintains that, at the time the simulants were sprayed, they were all known to be capable of causing illness or death.[46] Insisting that *Bacillus globigii* or BG (also known as *Bacillus subtilis*) is safe, the army has never carried out any health surveys of the populations targeted in its tests, before or after the tests have been done. Cole argues that BG can cause infections in people weakened by other conditions—the very old, the very young, people whose immune system has been compromised.[47] He points out that, in 1958, the army decided not to go ahead with BG trials because they could have involved exposing army personnel to levels of contamination that might have constituted a health hazard.

This was an explicit admission that BG can be dangerous: yet trials involving civilians continued, including one in the New York subway in 1966. *Serratia* is no longer used; but BG is still sprayed at the Dugway Proving Ground, 70 miles from Salt Lake City.

In 1955, the agent that causes Q-fever was sprayed from aeroplanes over the Dugway Proving Ground. Ten organisms are enough to infect a person with Q-fever, which is a debilitating condition whose symptoms can include chills, loss of appetite, pneumonia, pains in the chest and joints, fever and vomiting. Untreated, it will be fatal for up to 4 percent of people infected. Recovery prospects are good if treatment is prompt, but relapses can occur. The official document (released in 1994 in response to a Freedom of Information request) in which the test is described[48] recounts that "Guinea pigs were placed at the sampling stations. Results indicated that if human beings had been placed in the area, 99 percent of them would have been infected." If concentrations sufficient to cause this rate of infection were achieved inside the perimeter of the Proving Ground, it is legitimate to wonder how the agent was confined within the fence.

CHANGE OF POLICY

But US energy was not only going into BW research. The mid-sixties saw increasing public hostility to the use of chemical weapons in the Vietnam War. Scientists became involved, petitioning President Johnson for an end to this and a review of the country's chemical and biological warfare policies. In 1969, President Nixon renounced biological weapons—whether as a statesmanlike act or for US security reasons, is still debated. For a few years, support for research into the weapons declined.

Since the mid-1970s, it has revived again. This has happened in the context of President Reagan's suspicion of the Soviet Union, the "yellow rain" accusations and the increased funding that particular bandwagon managed to secure. Since the beginning of the 1980s, the focus has shifted again. Modern biotechnology makes it relatively easy for nations with only modest scientific capabilities to make their own biological weapons. This means there is a danger of proliferation: one of the worst nightmares of the superpowers, whose general belief in their own right to possess weapons of mass destruction is only equalled by their horror of others possessing them. Thus, the late eighties had seen a rise in military research and development in this field. Although still only a small fraction of the total US military budget, "support for research in the life sciences and medical defense under the Chemical Warfare and Biological Defense programs rose by about 400 percent in real terms . . . from 1980 to 1987."[49]

The American programme was extensive. But even before it began, Japan had not only developed but used biological weapons—as we will see in the next chapter.

GRUINARD

Gruinard Island is a rocky, heather-covered outcrop on the west coast of Scotland, one and a half miles long and a mile wide. It was requisitioned as a remote and safe place for discovering whether anthrax bombs would really kill. Sheep were the targets. They were tethered in various lines at specified distances from 4–lb bombs, which were suspended from gallows. The bombs contained a slurry of anthrax spores which, on firing, were released in an aerosol cloud which blew over the sheep. Sampling devices placed next to the sheep recorded what dose they inhaled. Afterwards, they were moved to an observation paddock where they died a few days later from pulmonary anthrax. The trials showed that the bombs killed nearly all sheep tethered up to 250 yards away—and that doses recorded 400 yards downwind would probably have been fatal. The dead sheep were pushed over a cliff, and explosives detonated to bring it down on top of them. The first test series ended on a beach at Penclawdd, the Welsh coast, with the bomb dropped from a Blenheim IV aircraft. An top secret official document released in 1999 records: "A stretch of sand near the mouth of an estuary and all land downwind from the crater was completely submerged by the tide a few hours after the trial. The whole area was thus effectively decontaminated." The next year, 1943, saw another series on Gruinard, testing bombs which could be incorporated into clusters.

Official documents show that the scientists acknowledged that the trials "must be recognised as dangerous both to personnel and the surrounding country." The casualties from this operation were, apart from the sheep on Gruinard, seven cattle, two horses, three cats and up to 50 sheep in a nearby village—all of which had probably been infected by a dog which had itself been infected by a sheep's carcass washed ashore from the island. John Bryden reports that one of the Canadians involved in biological weapons research during the War thought that some people had also been killed at Gruinard.[50]

After the trials came an attempt to rid the island of anthrax contamination. Burning the heather did not work. Annual samples from the island showed that, as late as 1968, the anthrax was still present in the soil. It was assumed that the whole island would need decontamination, and as nobody knew how to do it, the problem was put on one side. By 1979, the biological defence establishment at Porton Down (then known as the Chemical Defence Establishment, CDE) had developed a technique of finding out just how contaminated the soil was. CDE took over responsibility for Gruinard, and discovered that, far from the whole island needing decontamination, it would only be necessary on a limited area around the original test site and the animal observation paddock: a total area of 4.1 hectares.[51] After testing a short-list of chemicals that looked promising, CDE chose formaldehyde as the best for the job. The system chosen involved laying down irrigation tubing and spraying each of 46 treatment plots, one at a time, with a series of ten-minute sprays designed to be gentle enough to avoid run-off and erosion. The initial spraying took three weeks in the summer of 1986, after which the areas were sampled again. Analysis showed that nine of the 284 sites known to have been contaminated before the spraying still contained anthrax, so they were treated again with undiluted formalin. By October 1987, after 40 nonbreeding Cheviot ewes had been allowed to graze all over the island with no ill effects, these remaining sites too were pronounced clean. Gruniard was returned to civilian use in 1990—47 years after the tests.

BW IN THE LONDON UNDERGROUND

How fitting that the pub opposite Colliers Wood tube station should have a military theme. *The Victory,* with superb brass posts adorning its bar, celebrates Nelson's flagship at Trafalgar. It was another sort of defence, however, that London Transport workers were thinking about when they turned their backs on the pub and entered the station on 26 July, 1963. Their job was to release germs from a train, to see how they would be spread through the subway system.

At the bottom of the escalators the LT workers turned left onto the north-bound platform with its grey and green tiles: one of the dreariest sights on the Underground. But soon there was the distant rumble of an approaching train, a light glinting on the rails, and the grey front of the first carriage burst out of the tunnel.

The journey to the next station, Tooting Broadway, took just under two minutes. During that time, the two men dropped a small tin containing 30g of the bacterium *Bacillus globigii* onto the tracks. This was the same bacterium sprayed over cities in the US to see what would happen in a biological attack. The US army insisted publicly the bacterium was harmless, but it has been known to cause infections in the very old or very young, or people whose immune systems are already compromised. Internal documents show the US Army stopped using it in situations where its personnel would be exposed to high concentrations because it judged these might be "levels of contamination that would constitute a health hazard."

According to Brian Balmer, lecturer in Science Policy Studies at University College, London, samples collected from the Underground over the next twelve days showed that the bacterium had travelled as far as Camden Town, ten miles north.[52] Balmer cites the official conclusion: ". . . bacterial spores can be carried for several miles in the Tube system," and ". . . trains travelling through an aerosol become heavily contaminated internally."

This was not the first or last such experiment to be conducted in Britain. The Ministry of Defence has confirmed it carried out other secret tests in London and the south-east until at least 1977. In some trials simulants were dispersed on British Railways, in the London Post Office cable tunnel system, or sprayed into the air from a ship off Lyme Bay in Dorset. Other trials were done in central Southampton and at the biological defence establishment at Porton Down. There were also trials in the underground citadels of government buildings, which had shown that spores travel widely.

How did such trials help the country's defence? They probably did more to clarify a threat than suggest defensive measures. Balmer reports that only one official came up with a suggestion to thwart the spread of germs after an attack in the Underground—to close the floodgates in the tube system.

Similar trials were carried out in public places in America. In 1964, the US Army sprayed the same bacterium as a simulant for smallpox in the main waiting area of Washington's airport. The tests showed that passengers would have carried the infection to more than 200 cities.[53] In 1966, the Army distributed the bacterium throughout the New York subway system, dropped in a light bulb onto the track. Based on the level of contamination it caused, a real attack in a similar manner would have caused 12,000 cases of anthrax, 200,000 cases of tularemia or 300,000 cases of Q-fever.[54]

SABOTAGE?

Were the Germans waging biological warfare against the British? During World War II, it was the job of the Bacterial Sabotage Reference Library (BRSL) to find out. People were encouraged to send in anything suspicious which might indicate a biological attack. Mr P Bruce White, a bacteriologist with the BRSL, examined all the samples. The population willingly did their bit for the War effort, and Mr White was kept very busy.

One lady submitted something obviously suspicious: a white dust which mysteriously landed on her windowsill one morning. It turned out to be kapok knocked out of a mattress which her upstairs neighbour had flapped in the open air.

Anything unfamiliar thrown over hedges by small boys was assumed to have come from enemy aircraft—even in the country, where people saw "common objects of natural history" with new eyes. According to A Landsborough Thomson, official historian of the Medical Research Council, "many of the incidents merely illustrated the extent of human credulity and ignorance."

Mr White was obviously the man for the job. Landsborough Thomson writes: "Nobody could have been better fitted for the task; not only was he highly competent to discover any noxious factor in the specimen, but he enjoyed the detective role and persisted towards a complete identification of the object long after he knew it to be bacteriologically harmless. That most of the suspicions soon proved to be not only baseless but fanciful appealed to his appreciation of the absurd; he had indeed a strong sense of humour, so deadpan that one was often in doubt whether he was serious . . ."

Another scare concerned cobweb-like filaments discovered in the air in various places in 1940. These were analysed at Porton, which pronounced them innocent and naturally-occurring. In fact, a similar phenomenon had been observed by the eighteenth-century naturalist Gilbert White, who lived at Selbourne in Hampshire (Hants), and who described the airborne gossamer in one of his letters. This prompted an anonymous wit to write a ditty, "Gossamer," in September 1940:

"Security of home and health were shaking in their pants
Till Colville quoted a piece from White of Selbourne, Hants.
They sent it out on all the wires: 'This matter's quite alright
For any further references see letter, Gilbert White.' "
No evidence of enemy BW was ever found.[55]

BW AND THE BONE MAN

When War broke out, Sir Edward Mellanby was Secretary of the Medical Research Council. He could be called the guardian of the nation's bones, having discovered that rickets was caused by a lack of Vitamin D. During the War butter was rationed. Margarine, which was substituted for it, contained little of the precious Vitamin, but it was fortified with it on the basis of Mellanby's work. He also discovered that the flour used for baking bread during the War would reduce the body's absorption of calcium. (The reason was the unusually large amount of phytic acid in the flour, which used 85 percent of the grain instead of the 70 percent that pre-War white bread had used. Using the larger proportion meant that less wheat had to be imported, which enabled ships to carry more supplies vital to the War.) The remedy was simple: to add calcium to the flour. The official historian of the Medical Research Council, A Landsborough Thomson, comments: "This simple health-saving process was known to the obscurantists as 'putting chalk in our bread.' "

Mellanby accepted the job as Secretary of the MRC on condition that he could carry on with his own research. He believed that medical science should be used for the benefit of the population, and wanted to have nothing to do with research into biological weapons. In a lecture he gave at Manchester University on 17 June, 1943, he referred to "the prostitution and degradation of science, especially for the purposes of war." His view was well known: Landsborough Thomson, in his official history of the MRC, states that "The [Medical Research] Council did not wish to be concerned with the study of bacteriological warfare from an offensive angle, even although such methods would not be used except in retaliation—and granting that information of value for defensive purposes might be obtained." Mellanby continued his Manchester lecture by asserting, "If society is so arranged and the public mind so determines, scientific knowledge can be used so as to be wholly beneficial. Whatever the future holds in this respect it can be claimed that, even in wartime, medical research and its participants come to the bar with clean hands and that their work has, up to the present time, only conferred untold benefit upon mankind and has not been directed to his maiming and extermination." Whether he knew about the trials of anthrax bombs on Gruinard Island that had already been carried out, we do not know.[56]

WAS HEYDRICH ASSASSINATED BY BW?

On 27 May, 1942, just after 10.30am, Czech resistance fighter Jan Gabcik strode into the middle of a road in a suburb of Prague and took aim at Reinhard Heydrich's car as it came round a bend towards him. Heydrich was head of the Nazi security service and said to be the man Hitler wanted to succeed him. Gabcik and six other Czechs had been trained and equipped for the assassination by the British. At the crucial moment, when Gabcik tried to fire his sub-machine gun, it jammed. Mayhem ensued, with Heydrich screaming at his driver to drive on, and the driver hesitating. Jan Kubis, one of the other Czechs, hurled a grenade at Heydrich and wounded him. The German was rushed to hospital and operated on to remove dirt and splinters from his spleen. He was expected to recover, but his condition suddenly worsened and he died a week later.

The allegation that the grenade that killed Heydrich was actually filled with botulism, one of the most potent poisons known, was first made in 1971.[57] Since then, it has been reported that Paul Fildes, who headed the BW work at Porton, had boasted to some American microbiologists that he had "had a hand" in Heydrich's death.[58] If botulism was the cause, it would have been introduced into Heydrich on the bomb splinters that lodged in his spleen. The cause of death was said to be septicaemia, caused by "bacteria and possibly by poisons carried into [vital organs] by the bomb splinters."[59] However, an official report compiled by Heinz Pannwitz, chief of Gestapo department IIg which dealt with assassinations, illegal possession of weapons and sabotage, says that the fragments that penetrated his body carried with them parts of the horse-hair upholstery of the car seat, "thus causing the blood poisoning that resulted in Heydrich's death . . ."[60]

Intrigued by the accusation, Porton's historian G B Carter combed through the files looking for evidence of Fildes's involvement. He reports that Fildes did so some work with bot-

ulinum toxin and "the efficiency of contaminated metal fragments in producing lethal wounds"; but that work was done
after the assassination. As to Fildes allegedly telling the Americans that he had been involved, Carter concludes: "no evidence has been seen at Porton Down that either confirms or
explicitly contradicts [these statements] . . . Until further evidence emerges, the matter remains obscure."

Less obscure was the revenge the Nazis wreaked for Heydrich's death. Suspecting one of the assassins might have
come from the Czech village of Lidice, they executed its entire
population of 1,300 men, women and children, and burned
and bulldozed the village to rubble.

FEATHERS

One of the most bizarre biological weapons systems ever developed must the United States' cluster bomb filled with
turkey feathers. It was dreamed up in response to the US
Army's requirement, stated in 1947, for a biological anti-crop
weapon system. The feathers could retain up to about 80 percent of their own weight of rust spores, which would attack
the stems of wheat and rye. The Americans estimated that if
weather conditions were favourable, each cluster would result
in point infections over 130 square kilometers of crops, reducing their crop yield by about one-third. The system was ready
to be used in 1953.

Equally extraordinary was the way the clusters would be
delivered: by free-floating unmanned balloons. They would
have been let loose by special US Air Force strategic balloon
forces at five launching sites, which would between them
have carried 4,000 weapons to the target—presumably the
wheat fields of the Ukraine. This project had become a high
priority by late 1953, by which time it was using about one-
sixth of the BW munitions development budget.

Feathers gave way to aircraft spray tanks as the favoured
means of dispersing spores. It is not known whether either
method was ever used.[61]

BW IN RHODESIA

In 1979 and 1980, 182 people died of anthrax in Zimbabwe (then Rhodesia). Nearly 11,000 people were affected during the same period. In the previous 29 years only 334 human cases had been reported in the same area.

A confidential communication from a person inside the Rhodesian system has admitted that the anthrax outbreak was deliberate. The regime used anthrax to kill the cattle of tribesmen helping guerillas who came over the border. The communication states: "The use of Anthrax . . . was carried out in conjunction with psychological suggestion to the tribespeople that their cattle were sick and dying because of disease introduced into Zimbabwe from Mozambique by the infiltrating guerillas."[62]

The same source asserted that the Rhodesian Security Forces had used cholera to contaminate watering points close to guerilla camps in Mozambique. However, the source continued, "this tactic was said to be of very limited use due to the quick dispersion of the bacteria."

The outbreaks of anthrax struck six of Zimbabwe's eight provinces. But hardly any commercial white farms were affected. The disease was almost entirely confined to the Tribal Trust Lands, now known as Communal Lands.

As a result of this biological warfare, anthrax is now endemic in Zimbabwe. From the beginning of 1981 to the end of 1985, a further 4,124 human cases were reported.

UK TRIALS

In the 1960s, during the Cold War, the UK Ministry of Defence was worried about a possible BW attack by the former Soviet Union. The MoD wanted to discover how far micro-organisms released as an aerosol would travel, so it carried out controlled releases of simulants from a ship, the *Icewhale*, off the south coast of England. Two organisms were used: *Bacillus globigii* (BG) and *E. coli 162*. They were picked up by monitoring stations about 80 miles apart: at Bournemouth in Dorset and Newton Abbot in Devon.

According to the the MoD, both simulants were thought to be harmless. It has since admitted that BG can affect immuno-suppressed people: the very old, the very young and those already ill. In fact the Americans had stopped using it as a simulant in their own dispersal tests by 1958, as they had become worried about its effects on their service personnel. The *E.coli* was tested on mice to see if it made them ill; but protesters today point out that the mice were not allowed to breed and therefore the MoD could not have known whether the organism had the potential to cause birth defects.

One of the villages in the range of the *Icewhale* tests was East Lulworth. Its inhabitants quote significantly raised rates of miscarriages and birth defects in women, and children born to them, during the test period. In August 1998, the MoD appointed an independent microbiologist to review the trials.

6

GERMANY, USSR, JAPAN AND SOUTH AFRICA

What were German researchers doing crawling around the scenic fields near Speyer in the Rhineland, in October 1943? They were looking for Colorado beetles—14,000 of the black and yellow pests, which had been dropped from a German plane. It must have been a frustrating day. They found only 57.[1]

Their hunt was part of an experiment in preparation for dropping the beetles onto potato crops in Eastern England. Colorado beetles (*Leptinotarsa decemlineata*—also known as potato bugs and potato weevils) devour potatoes, and the Germans estimated they might be able to reduce food calories available to the British by six percent. But they needed to know how they would be dispersed from an airdrop. They tried again, over the Rhineland fields, with wooden beetles painted so they would be easily seen. They hardly recovered more then either.

The beetle incident illustrates several characteristics about BW.

First, the Germans' motivation for doing BW work at all. They had worked to combat the Colorado beetle since 1935, when it had threatened as a naturally-occurring pest to cross into Germany from France and Belgium. Their defence interest was only awakened in 1940 when occupying German forces in France inspected laboratories at Le Bouchet. They found evidence of French BW work, including the dissemination of plant diseases and records of at least one incident in which the French had considered using Colorado beetles over enemy potato fields. The Germans became more alarmed when intelligence agents informed them of American Chemical Warfare Service experiments with potato beetles and

Texas ticks at the Edgewood Arsenal. This was followed, in April 1942, by another agent, working in England, reporting that 15,000 Colorado beetles had arrived from the United States in a B-24 Liberator aircraft. (It also carried Texas ticks, but the Germans judged them not to pose a danger to Germany, and lost interest in them.) But the Germans were afraid that the British were planning to use the beetle to attack German food supplies. They hastily assembled all their accumulated knowledge about defending themselves.

Intelligence reports, now known to be faulty, played a major role in German defensive preparations. It now seems that inaccurate intelligence reports largely accounted for the existence of other BW programmes as well.

During World War I, German agents had carried out sabotage operations against horses and cattle being shipped from US ports to the Allies. They inoculated horses with glanders, which produced high mortality rates, and contaminated cattle feed with anthrax spores. They also evaluated and rejected proposals to use anti-personnel agents against England.[2] The French had also conducted anti-animal BW sabotage, which may have been triggered by the Germans' activities. France and the Soviet Union took note of the Germans' sabotage, as well as "their knowledge of the extensive German use of chemical weapons in World War I and the perception of the high standard of German bacteriology"[3] and decided it all added up to a German BW threat. By the mid-1920s they had established their own programmes.

In the light of intelligence about the French and Soviet activities, the Germans themselves considered a BW programme but didn't go ahead with it. But again there were intelligence reports of a German programme; and in 1934, the English journalist Wickham Steed published "what purported to be reports of a series of *Reichswehrministerium* experiments conducted in 1932 in the field of BW."[4] His reports were exaggerated; but the effect of the available information was to encourage the British to establish their own programme, which they did in 1940. The Canadians, meanwhile, had become interested; and their programme, and that of the British and later the Americans, became closely intertwined. In 1940 the Germans' discoveries at Le Bouchet led to more intense activity in Germany, but still no offensive programme.

Dr Benjamin Garrett, of the Battelle Memorial Institute in Maryland, USA, speculates that the entire World War II potato beetle episode may have been caused by some innocent beetles found on the south coast of England in 1941. They were the subject of a "Most Secret" memorandum from Lord Hankey to Churchill on 6 December of that year, in which Hankey confides his suspicions of the Germans ("I would not trust the Germans, if driven to desperation, not to resort to such methods . . .")[5]—in spite of the fact that few potatoes were grown in the district and "no containers or other suspicious objects were discovered." But there were, said Hankey, "abnormal features in at least one instance suggesting that the occurrence was not due to natural causes."[6]

Garrett notes that Hankey finished his memo by asking for permission for preparatory measures against such BW attacks. It was granted on 2 January 1942. The plane load of beetles which aroused the Germans' suspicions arrived three months later. If it was part of the "preparatory measures" authorised in January, the German effort, with its experiments near Speyer, might have been built on the backs of some innocent beetles who strayed close to the sea.

Erhard Geissler and John Ellis van Courtland Moon have edited a weighty study of the history of BW programmes. They conclude: "The BTW programmes of the major belligerents were fuelled largely by their respective intelligence perceptions at the time . . . there was a widespread appreciation that everyone else was preparing for BTW . . . Only now is it clear that intelligence was inaccurate and incorrect."[7] Thus perceptions and suspicions led to preparations for biological war.

The other aspect of the potato beetle saga which illustrates current worries about BW programmes is the difficulty of distinguishing between defensive and offensive work.

When the German soldiers went hunting for documents at Le Bouchet, the Germans had no offensive programme. Hitler was informed of the preparations the Germans assumed the enemy was making, but he forbade use of BW against England, decreeing instead that defensive work should be intensified. Although Hitler was allegedly in favor of BW in the early 1930s, he was consistently opposed to any offensive BW activity during the Second World War. None of the records of the time spell out why; but Professor

Erhard Geissler, Head of the Bioethical Research Group at the Max-Delbruck Center for Molecular Medicine in Berlin, thinks it was probably because he was afraid of retaliation in kind and also felt bound to adhere to the Geneva Protocol. Germany had ratified it without reservation, and Hitler only considered leaving it in February, 1945, as a result of the Anglo-American fire-bombing of Dresden. In fact, Germany did not renounce its ratification.

In 1940, then, the order went down to the German scientists involved in beetle research that offensive work was prohibited. Nevertheless, the German High Command agreed that defensive work would require knowledge of how an attack might be made: "it is necessary that we carry out experiments. You have to attack yourself before you can judge protective measures correctly."[8] The word was passed to the scientists that "in order to give suitable protection regulations, the enemy's technique of introduction must be tested. Therefore the experiments planned are not at variance with the Fuhrer's order."[9]

According to Geissler, the defensive programme quickly slipped into offensive mode, and the scientists estimated that 20–40 million beetles would be needed to destroy 400,000 hectares of English potato fields. By June, 1943, they were breeding beetles in two stations in Western France, where they occurred naturally. Delivery trials were carried out in October (nobody seems to have considered the possibility that they meant that Germany was waging BW on itself), and the forecast was that there would be enough beetles for attacks against England by the summer of 1944.[10]

Geissler comments: "the history of potato beetles as BW agents demonstrates the difficulty in assessing the intentions of studies and even field trials of dual-threat agents."[11] The same problem is still with us today.

In spite of the very low recovery rate, the dispersal experiments did not deter the scientists. The results were "variously interpreted as indicative of either very effective, large-scale dispersal (i.e. only a few were recovered because the rest had travelled far away, and that was good) or, conversely, rather ineffective dispersal."[12]

In June 1944, the High Command was informed that the beetle could be used at any time. It seems they never were. After the War, however, there was an outbreak of Colorado beetles in East Germany. The East German government accused the Americans of dropping the beetles from planes flying over the country, but there was never any evidence to support the allegation.

These days there are effective pesticides which deal with the Colorado beetle. They are no longer regarded as a threat.

The work on the Colorado beetle was part of a very small German BW research effort during the Second World War. Geissler quotes an opinion that only about twenty people were involved. As well as the beetle experiments, they studied the usefulness of the foot-and-mouth virus and whether mustard gas would make anthrax more effective. "During World War II," says Geissler, "biological and toxin weapon agents were not used by Germany either as offensive or as retaliatory weapons."

The German authorities have opened their archives, allowing scholars to trace the development of Germany's biological weapons activities.[13] The same cannot be said for the Soviet Union. However, details of its extensive programme have recently been revealed.

THE USSR

The Allies learned about Soviet developments from German and Japanese sources after the Second World War. A Japanese Colonel Masuda questioned by the Allies said that five Russian spies had been caught in Japanese-occupied Manchuria with glass ampules containing organisms producing dysentery, cholera and anthrax. He claimed that this and other similar captures stimulated the Japanese to start their own BW programme:[14] a hopeful attempt to deceive, as Japanese activities had started independently of any others.

Captured German army files included reports from Russian prisoners and defectors that the Soviets had begun work on BW during the thirties. There were accounts of field stations at which tests were meant to have been carried out, including some in 1937 on Vozrozhdeniya Island in the Aral Sea. One deserter, called Von Apen, even alleged that Soviet scientists had experimented upon human subjects in Mongolia, in 1941. According to Von Apen, political prisoners and Japanese prisoners of war were confined to a tent with plague-infested rats until they had been bitten by the rats' fleas. Von Apen said that one prisoner, who had escaped, had set off an epidemic of plague in which between three and five thousand Mongols died.[15] Statements made by Soviet officials as early as 1938 threatened that the nation would respond in kind to any BW attack: a Soviet General was reported by the *New York Times* to this effect on 23 February, 1938. In 1956, Marshal Zhukov told the Twentieth Party Congress that the Soviet Union expected future war to be waged with various weapons of mass destruction, including bacteriological ones. Although he did not spell out any Soviet BW capacity, the implication was that it would not be found wanting.

The Russian Federation is a party to the 1972 Biological Weapons Convention which bans the development, production or stockpiling of BW. The late 1970s, however, saw the start of various accusations that the Soviets were indeed developing biological weapons.

The first of these concerned an outbreak of anthrax in April, 1979 in Sverdlovsk (now Ekaterinburg), about 900 miles east of Moscow. Russian emigres in Frankfurt alleged that hundreds of people had been killed in an accident involving anthrax.[16] The Americans suggested the anthrax had been accidentally released from a military facility. The Soviets denied this, saying that anthrax-contaminated meat had been to blame. The second allegation was that the Soviets were supplying toxin to troops waging warfare in Southeast Asia (see below).

The nature of the anthrax accident was disputed for years, with Soviet and American positions being buttressed by statements from people in the area at the time, underground sources of information, official allegations and even a presentation to the US National Academy of Sciences by Soviet doctors who had treated the victims. The matter was not resolved until 1992, when President Yeltsin admitted that it had indeed been an outbreak from a military biological facility: Military Camp 19 in Sverdlovsk, which was in 1979 working on an anthrax vaccine. Early in 1998, a joint team of Russian and American scientists examined tissue from samples from the victims and were able to identify strains of anthrax which confirmed that they were not from natural sources.

The outbreak, which in fact killed 68 people, was a shocking reminder of the lethality of biological weapons. It seems that only a small fraction of a gram of spores was released, yet this was enough to kill people over a wide area.

At the beginning of 1992, President Yeltsin promised to stop Russian research on biological weapons. In the months that followed, the Russians made other disclosures about their BW programme. They confirmed that they had held field tests of BW agents on Vozrozhdeniye Island, and that bacteriological research had been done in various other locations in Moscow, Leningrad and Novosibirsk. Anatoly Kuntsevich, then in charge of the government committee on BW, admitted that the Soviet Union's research into BW had not stopped after it ratified the Biological Weapons Convention: "there were, legally speaking, violations of it in this country," he said. The USSR had continued research, testing and production of BW, including ways of delivering them.[17] An article in *Izvestia* in June 1993 gave a fuller description of the programme: "Production tasks were offered to a large industrial complex, '*Biopreparat*,' which had production facilities all over the country . . . Eighteen R&D Institutes having 25 thousand staff, 6 plants and a large warehouse in Siberia were included into the System . . . The Institute in Kol'tsovo near Novosibirsk worked on the lethal virus of haemorrhagic fever and on Venezuela [equine] encephalitis. Experiments needed for testing plague and malignant anthrax were conducted in Obolensk. In Leningrad, experiments were conducted on tularemia . . ."[18]

Defectors' revelations

Defectors from the former Soviet Union's bioweapons programme have revealed just how big the effort was. Microbiologist Vladimir Pasechnik arrived in the United Kingdom in 1989, having been director of the Institute of Ultrapure Biopreparations in Leningrad. He was interviewed by British intelligence, which concluded that part of his work was to develop a strain of the plague bacterium, *Yersinia pestis,* that was resistant to antibiotics. Thoroughly alarmed, the British and the Americans briefed Prime Minister

Thatcher and President Bush on Pasechnik's revelations. They put pressure on President Gorbachev to allow British and American inspectors into Biopreparat plants.

In January 1991 the inspectors went into plants near Novosibirsk and Obolensk. The visits were an exercise in Soviet duplicity. The Soviet host was Dr Kanatjan Alibekov, the First Deputy Chief of Biopreparat. He has since admitted: "The main purpose during all [the] preparatory period was to hide all information that could be considered offensive information, because all of these facilities were strictly offensive facilities." One of the British inspectors was Dr David Kelly, Senior Adviser on Biological Defence to the Ministry of Defence. He says the Russian deception was quite elaborate: "they had in place a system whereby they had an apparently civilian programme embedded in civilian industry which was contributing directly to the military programme of Russia . . . It was obviously a deception that had been well considered and well planned in advance. It was not something that was undertaken on the spur of the moment." And another British inspector, Dr Christopher Davis, who occupied the BW desk of the Defence Intelligence Staff, adds: "Finding the truth was like grabbing a bar of soap in the shower."

Reciprocal Russian inspections of American facilities followed in December 1991. The Russian scientists went to the US Army Medical Research Institute of Infectious Diseases (USAMRIID) at Fort Detrick, the Army's Dugway Proving Ground in Utah, and Pine Bluff in Arkansas where the Army used to store biological weapons. They found no evidence of a continuing programme: at Pine Bluff, the rusted railway tracks and unkempt buildings were eloquent testimony to the abandonment of the offensive BW effort years before. Dr Alibekov was part of the Russian team. "I found out there was no . . . offensive programme in the US," he says. This came as a shock. Russian scientists had never believed that the US had in fact stopped its military programme. But what awaited the Russians on their return home was even worse. They were told that it didn't matter whether the Americans were pursuing an offensive programme or not. Their report, remembers Alibekov, was to "find any evidence to prove the existence of such a programme in the United States."

This so disgusted Alibekov that he left Biopreparat. He managed to move his family to the United States, where he now lives as Dr Kenneth Alibek. He has revealed that he had 32,000 scientists and staff working under him in Biopreparat facilities across the Soviet Union. Biopreparat was set up in 1973—the year after the Soviet Union signed the Biological Weapons and Convention, promising to stop offensive BW work—to research and produce both vaccines and biological weapons. Alibek himself made a super-strong kind of anthrax. He confirms that, by 1991, Soviet scientists were testing the dissemination of plague bacteria engineered to be immune to antibiotics. The Soviets had picked out the targets for the warheads they had designed to be filled with anthrax, smallpox and plague: London, Los Angeles, New York and Washington DC. They had made large quantities of the Marburg virus, replicating it from the blood, liver and spleen of an unfortunate colleague who was accidentally infected with it and died in April, 1988. They had used their stock of smallpox, entrusted to them by the World Health Organisation after the global eradication of the disease, to produce large amounts of the virus for biological weapons. Because smallpox has been beaten, people no longer have any immunity to it. Alibek says that they also engineered a combination of smallpox and Ebola.

Alibek has also revealed that the Soviet Union began to develop anti-agricultural biological weapons in the late 1940s. At a meeting in Washington in September 1998, he explained that the code name for this programme was "Ecology," and that it involved three categories of weapons: anti-crop, anti-livestock and combined anti-personnel/anti-livestock. "The anti-crop agents included wheat rust, rice blast and rye blast; the anti-livestock weapons included African swine fever, Rinderpest and foot-and-mouth disease; and the combined antipersonnel/anti-livestock agents included anthrax and psittacosis," he said. In contrast to the anti-personnel weapons however, the fruits of "Ecology" were never produced on a regular basis or stockpiled. Instead, a number of facilities were equipped to convert to weapons production rapidly, should the need arise. According to Alibek, work on them stopped in 1990 because the military planners did not consider them strategic weapons.

As Alibek pointed out, however, this does not mean that animals would be unaffected in future conflicts. Anti-personnel biological weapons infect animals too. Anthrax is also fatal to cattle, sheep and goats; brucellosis can also be lethal in livestock. Venezuelan equine encephalitis incapacitates humans but kills horses, as does glanders. According to Alibek, the Soviet Union had actually used glanders as biological weapons in Afghanistan to both sicken the mujaheddin and kill their horses, which they relied on for transport in the mountains.

YELTSIN

When President Yeltsin took over in 1992, he admitted the existence of the offensive BW programme and said it was run by "fanatics." The declared aim is now to convert it to civilian industry. Anthony Rimmington, at the Centre for Russian and East European Studies at the University of Birmingham, judges that by prohibiting further BW development, and by opening Russian facilities to inspectors from the UK and US, the Yeltsin administration wants to "present itself as adhering to international norms with the aim of reintegrating the Russian Federation within the world community. It is also a reflection of the government's overall conversion programme which as part of the transition to a market economy aims to severely reduce military production."[19] There is however no guarantee that the "fanatics" are still not producing their wares behind the Government's back. Dr Alibek says the Russians are still cheating.

The Soviet biological warfare programme not only developed anti-personnel agents. There was also an extensive anti-agricultural effort. This is described in Chapter Seven.

It seems that the Soviet programme was originally influenced by perceptions of German activities in World War I. To some degree, developments in France, Germany, the Soviet Union and Britain and her allies were mutually influenced—at least initially—by their perceptions of the others' work. One country stood outside these mutual influences. That was the country whose biological war crimes are in a league of their own: Japan.

JAPAN

"In January 1945 . . . I saw experiments in inducing gas gangrene, conducted under the direction of the Chief of the 2nd Division, Colonel Ikari, and researcher Futaki. Ten prisoners . . .

were tied facing stakes, five to ten meters apart . . . The prisoners' heads were covered with metal helmets, and their bodies with screens . . . only the naked buttocks being exposed. At about 100 meters away a fragmentation bomb was exploded by electricity . . . All ten men were wounded . . . and sent back to prison . . . I later asked Ikari and researcher Futaki what the results had been. They told me that all ten men had . . . died of gas gangrene."[20]

So testified one witness at the Khabarovsk War Crimes Trial in 1949. Twelve Japanese soldiers were prosecuted by the Russians for biological warfare crimes. The trial recorded some of the atrocities of Japan's occupation of Manchuria, the northeastern part of China, between 1931 and 1945.

As far as is known, Japan is the only country which has carried out systematic BW experiments on live human beings. Just as the British preferred to experiment with chemical weapons in their former colonies rather than on home ground,[21] the Japanese also thought their BW work too sensitive to be carried out in their own country. Their programme was highly organised and spread over nineteen facilities. One of the main headquarters was in a suburb of the city of Harbin called Ping Fan, which by 1940 employed 3,000 people. British intelligence documents report a post-War American assessment that the Japanese "developed a biological warfare organization that at its height extended from Harbin to the Dutch East Indies and from the island of Hokkaido to the Celebes."[22]

The moving force behind the Japanese programme was Lt. General Ishii Shiro. Clever, arrogant, ambitious, and known for his drinking and womanising, Ishii was a medical doctor with a PhD in microbiology at the Tokyo Army Medical School. Ironically, his interest in BW was stimulated by the 1925 Geneva Protocol which outlawed "bacteriological methods of warfare." If it was worth banning, Ishii thought, it must be a potentially valuable weapon. Using his assiduously tended contacts in the army and academia, he lobbied for the initiation of BW research. He was allowed to begin it in Tokyo in 1932, but was conscious that he could not experiment on people there. Later the same year he travelled to Manchuria, where he set up a laboratory in Harbin and built a camp for human experiment at an isolated village called Beiyinhe.

By 1937, when he abandoned it for the bigger facility he ordered built at Ping Fan, his methods were well established.[23]

His subjects were a mixture of anti-Japanese activists, common criminals and some innocents who were picked up in police round-ups. Ishii wanted to infect them with various diseases and monitor how they reacted. At Beiyinhe he concentrated on anthrax, glanders and plague. Sheldon Harris, Emeritus Professor of History at California State University, whose book *Factories of Death* is the most widely researched and recent examination of these crimes, recounts: "One was an early test performed on three communist guerrillas. Ishii prepared for the test by commandeering forty mice that were captured in a natural plague area along the Manchuria-Soviet border. Some fleas were lured from the mice, and a bacterium produced from the plague-infested fleas was injected into the prisoners. All three victims were soon delirious with fever. On the twelfth day, one guerilla was observed with a temperature of 40 degrees Celsius. Another's fever was recorded as 39 degrees Celsius on the nineteenth day of his ordeal. There is no record for the third patient. However, all three were dissected while unconscious."[24] When they were no longer needed for experiments, or judged too weak for them (sometimes after prolonged taking of blood), the prisoners were poisoned or shot, and cremated.

Harris again: "If Ishii or one of his co-workers wished to do research on the human brain, then they would order the guards to find them a useful sample. A prisoner would be taken from his cell. Guards would hold him while another guard would smash the victim's head open with an axe. His brain would be extracted and rushed immediately to the laboratory. The body would then be whisked off to the pathologist, and then to the crematorium for the usual disposal."[25]

The experiments continued at Ping Fan and other bases, and broadened to include botulism, brucellosis, meningococcus, encephalitis, cholera, typhoid, paratyphoid A and B, typhus, smallpox, tularemia, infectious jaundice, gas gangrene, tetanus, dysentery, scarlet fever, undulant fever, gangrene, tuberculosis, salmonella, frostbite and yellow fever. The cold winters gave plenty of opportunity to experiment with frostbite. Nishi Toshihide, who observed some of these experiments, described them after the war: "At times of great frost, with temperatures below −20 Celsius, people were brought out from the detachment's prison into the open. Their arms were bared and made to freeze with the help of an artificial current of air. This was done until their frozen arms, when struck with a short stick, emitted a sound resembling that which a board gives out when it is struck."[26] They were then taken inside and subjected to various efforts to defrost them, so that the Japanese could learn the best way of dealing with frostbite.

Experiments on humans formed one part of the BW programme. The Japanese also wanted to learn how best to disseminate disease. They investigated different methods, from artillery shells which did not spread their bacterial payload in the desired way, to bombs designed to burst above the ground, spewing out plague-infested fleas. These, too, were unsuccessful: the fleas, reportedly made sluggish by the high temperatures produced when the bombs exploded, evidently failed to infect the hapless humans tethered to stakes on the target area. Pingfan was said to be able to produce 500 million fleas a year.

The list of atrocities goes on and on. Harris concludes that the true number of victims will never be known. They almost certainly run into tens of thousands. They include prisoners killed in experiments at Ping Fan (by Japanese admission, 3,000 alone between 1941 and the end of the war) and others in other bases not directly under Ishii's control. They also include all the prisoners killed by the Japanese in order to silence them, as the camp staffs retreated before the Russian advance in 1945. At Hailar, for example, the Russians found one shallow grave containing 10,000 Chinese and Mongolian men, women and children—many of the bodies still warm. Harris reminds us that the total death toll must also include the people around Ping Fan who died in plague epidemics in 1946, '47 and '48: 30,000 people in the '47 epidemic alone. Plague had not broken out in the region before, and Chinese doctors became convinced that it was spread by infected animals let loose by the retreating Japanese in 1945: by some of the rats, mice, rabbits, guinea pigs, cattle, sheep, goats, mules, donkeys and even some camels used in the programme.[27]

There have been allegations that Allied prisoners of war were also experimented on. The Mukden camp held British, American,

Australian and New Zealand prisoners; and British journalists Peter Williams and David Wallace claimed in their book *Unit 731*[28] that the Japanese wanted to see how men of different racial origins would react to pathogens. Williams and Wallace believe the Japanese monitored the prisoners to chronicle the effects of quasi-malnutrition, and suggest that they made them drink liquids infected with cholera and dysentery.[29] The diaries of Mukden inmates record that they were given what they were told were inoculations against dysentery, cholera, typhoid, smallpox and tetanus; that rectal smears were taken from time to time, and that medical examinations were carried out. Dysentery was rife amongst the prisoners and many Americans died.

Was this experimentation? Williams and Wallace say yes. Harris is not convinced. His main reason for doubt is that the prisoners who were still alive in Mukden at the end of the war were not killed by the Japanese—unlike the inmates of all the other camps in which they had done BW experiments on humans.[30]

Part of the difficulty in establishing exactly what went on at Mukden stems from the lack of investigation immediately after the war. The Americans, however, had good reason not to inquire too closely into what happened.

The Americans wrote a scandalous footnote to this obscene Japanese chapter. At the end of the war they discovered that the Japanese had experimented on people, but they gave Ishii and the rest immunity from prosecution in order to learn the results of their experiments. The American attitude was summed up by Edwin V. Hill, M.D., Chief of Basic Sciences at Camp Detrick—the headquarters of the Americans' BW research. In 1947, he wrote that the data gathered by Japanese scientists "has greatly supplemented and amplified previous aspects of this field . . . Information has accrued with respect to human susceptibility to these diseases as indicated by specific infectious doses of bacteria. Such information could not be obtained in our own laboratories because of scruples attached to human experimentation . . . It is hoped that individuals [i.e., Japanese scientists interrogated by the Americans] who voluntarily contributed this information will be spared embarrassment because of it . . ."[31] The Japanese only opened up to the Americans about the experiments after they had been assured they would not be prosecuted. Comments Harris: "No one . . . was prepared to raise the issue of ethics, or morality, or traditional Western or Judo-Christian human values in confronting those responsible [for agreeing to grant immunity to the Japanese]. The question of ethics and morality as they affected scientists in Japan and the United States never once entered into a single discussion that is recorded in any of the minutes, notes, records of meetings, etc. . . . In all the considerable documentation that has survived over the more than four decades from the events described, not one individual is chronicled as having said BW human experiments were an abomination, and that their perpetrators should be prosecuted. The only concern voiced was that of the possibility that exposure would cause the United States some embarrassent, should word of the bargain become public knowledge."[32]

Most of the Japanese scientists who experimented on humans were never called to account. Harris finds it hard to explain why the Chinese, who had suffered most at their hands, did not pursue them after the war; but wonders whether the Americans and the Russians, both of whom wanted to know about the Japanese experiments, persuaded their friends in China (the Kuomintang and the Communists) not to raise the issue. In 1949, in Khabarovsk, the Russians did prosecute twelve Japanese for BW crimes. They were all found guilty but received comparatively lenient sentences.

Writing in 1989, Wallace and Williams summarise what happened after the war to the Japanese scientists: "Protected by the deal struck between General MacArthur and their leaders, they resumed their places in a reconstructed Japanese society and were, and are, numbered among the most senior and respected names in the Japanese scientific community."[33]

SOUTH AFRICA

After the apartheid era ended in South Africa in 1994, Archbishop Desmond Tutu set up the Truth and Reconciliation Commission which heard evidence of human rights abuses during the white regime. In 1998, the hearings revealed details of a chemical and biological weapons programme previously unknown. Code-named Project Coast, it was headed by cardiologist and personal physician to former President P W Botha, Dr Wouter Basson. He only appeared before the Commission after the government failed in a bid to have him and his colleagues give evidence in secret.

Project Coast was located within the army's special forces and staffed almost entirely by doctors. It carried out research on ways of killing people by means that would make their deaths seem natural. The Commission was shown various assassination instruments designed to achieve this: needle tubes which could be loaded into an umbrella or walking stick and used to inject poison into a victim; other sprung devices which fired a tiny ball of poison into a victim; chocolates filled with cyanide, cholera and anthrax; and envelopes and cigarettes spiked with cholera and anthrax. The Project had produced whisky mixed with paraquat, mamba venom, and deodorant contaminated with typhoid. One participating laboratory, the Roodeplaat Research Laboratory near Pretoria, had issued, among other items, 32 bottles of cholera germs, cyanide, thallium, anthrax, botulism and salmonella.

The apartheid regime had used these agents in many assassination attempts, some of which were successful. Dr Schalk van Rensburg, a veterinarian who did research at the Roodeplaat Research Laboratory, confirmed to the Commission that security services had tried to murder three Russian advisers to the African National Council by dosing their food with anthrax. One of them died.

One of the most sinister elements of the biological weapons programme was described to the Commission by the managing director of the Roodeplaat Research Laboratory, Dr Daan Goosen. He related that the South African military attache in London had been given a document anonymously in 1983 or 1984, offering a technique of developing a bacterium "which has got the possibility of only making sick and killing pigmented people." Basson ordered Goosen to investigate whether this would be scientifically feasible. Goosen concluded "it is a definite possibility," and "it was decided it would be good if the government had this as a weapon . . . as a negotiating back-up—to know what your strength is, what you can do in a crisis situation." In the event, however, the anonymous offer was not taken up because the South Africans feared it might be a trap.

Dr Goosen was not left without work, however. Basson wanted him to find a way of reducing black women's fertility, and research to develop a suitable vaccine formed his main project at Roodeplaat. Goosen says he told Basson that such a vaccine could not be made to work on black women only, but that Basson nevertheless ordered him to continue.

The chemical weapons programme was both horrifying and bizarre. Van Rensburg testified that Basson had told him that the black consciousness leader Steve Biko, who died in police custody, had been given the heavy metal poison thallium. This could have accounted for Biko's irrationally aggressive behaviour which the police countered with violence which killed him. Van Rensburg believed that there had been plans to poison Nelson Mandela with thallium, while he was in prison. He also said they tried to murder the former secretary-general of the South African Council of Churches, Dr Frank Chikane, by dusting his underpants with phosphates that would seep into his skin and trigger a heart attack. Chikane was only saved because, instead of travelling to Namibia as the security forces had expected, he went to America, where doctors were able to treat him.

A former professor of organic chemistry, Johan Koekemoer, testified that they had produced "huge quantities" of the drugs ecstasy and the sedative mandrax for the military. The former head of the police forensic laboratories, General Lothar Neethling, said he had supplied Basson with enough LSD to "put 50,000 men on a trip," as well as mandrax and 250 kilograms of marijuana. They were allegedly to be used in riot control—but never were. Another possible use which has been mooted for them was to feed them into townships to destabilise black communities.

The fact that South Africa had such a well-established chemical and biological weapons programme raises questions about how much other countries knew about it, and how much they might have helped in its development. Basson told the Commission that he "had good access to senior government officials and people" in Western countries in the early 1980s. He said that British, US, German, Japanese and Canadian experts had provided "incredible detail" about their biological weapons programmes, often in return for information about chemical weapons in Soviet-backed African countries. "I had access to very senior people," he said. Lieutenant

General Niels Knobel, former surgeon-general of the South African Defence Force, has asserted that South Africa received secret manuals "either stolen or given to us" from Porton Down. It is hard to imagine that Western officials, if they did give information to Basson, did not know what he would use it for. Or were they really shocked, as alleged by Mike Kennedy, the SA National Intelligence Agency's chief director for counter intelligence organisations, to discover the true extent of the programme in 1993/94?

From the evidence that emerged before the Truth and Reconciliation Commission, it seems that the immanence of democracy in South Africa in 1994 concentrated British and American minds. Officials from those countries are said to have contacted the dying apartheid regime expressing concern about what would happen to Project Coast's chemical and biological weapons. According to Basson and du Preez, the Western governments did not want the incoming ANC government to have access to them. Says Max du Preez, who edited a weekly South African TV programme on the Truth Commission: ". . . it was fine for the racist minority white government to have chemical and biological weapons, but not for the democratically elected black government . . . Can anybody blame us if we ask why the US has imposed sanctions and indeed war on Iraq and Libya because they allegedly have biological and chemical warfare programmes, but did not utter a word when the apartheid regime did the same?"

The biological weapons programmes described in the last two chapters varied in their extent and belligerence. All however depended on the same theoretical and experimental scientific knowledge: knowledge whose growing sophistication is another factor in the increasing fears about biological weapons. It is to this science that we turn in the next chapter.

YELLOW RAIN

American allegations that Soviet-backed forces were using toxicological warfare in South-East Asia must rank amongst the most bizarre episodes of international relations. First made by Secretary of State Alexander Haig in September, 1981, and described in more detail in November of that year by the State Department's Richard Burt, the accusations were that planes were spreading a yellow material that fell like rain over people in Laos, Kampuchea and Afghanistan. These people "would experience an early onset of violent itching, vomiting, dizziness, and distorted vision. Within a short time they would vomit blood tinged with material, then large quantities of bright red blood. Within an hour, they would die of apparent shock and massive loss of blood from the stomach."[34] Reports of the attacks came mainly from Hmong tribespeople from Laos who were living in Thai refugee camps. From 1979 on, The US State Department sent people to interview them and to gather samples of the material—yellow spots a few millimeters in diameter, on leaves and pieces of bark. An early sample was analysed at the University of Minnesota, which found a toxin which could account for the symptoms described. The toxin was a mycotoxin—i.e., produced by a fungus—that had never been known as a BW agent; but the coincidence seemed compelling. In September, 1981, Alexander Haig announced in Berlin the US had "physical evidence" of toxin warfare, which had "been analyzed and found to contain abnormally high levels of three potent mycotoxins—poisonous substances not indigenous to the region and which are highly toxic to man and animals."[35] As time went on, however, things appeared less simple. Only a few of the samples were said to contain the toxins; and even in these samples the toxins made up only a tiny amount of the whole. Although various US government laboratories tried to find out what the rest of the samples consisted of, it was not until 1982that scientists at Porton Down in England came up with the answer. It was pollen. The finding was quickly confirmed by laboratories all over the world.

The US administration accepted the evidence but argued that the Soviets had deliberately added the pollen to the toxin to make the weapon more effective. Sharon Watson, at the US Army Medical Intelligence and Information Agency at Fort Detrick, thought that the pollen and toxin had been mixed with a solvent which would make more toxin go through the skin. She called it "a very clever mixture." A different explanation for the presence of pollen came from Thomas Seeley at

Yale University, an expert on honeybees. He suggested it was the faeces of wild honeybees. Tests on the pollen showed it to be "empty husks, like those digested by honeybees ... Analyses done at the Smithsonian Institution in Washington and in other laboratories specialising in pollen identification in France, Great Britain and the United States showed that the pollen in yellow-rain samples was from plants indigenous to Southeast Asia and was composed of precisely the kind of pollen gathered and eaten by wild honeybees in the region's forests."[36] But what about the toxins found in the early sample? As analytical methods became more sophisticated, they failed to find toxins in nearly all the samples still coming in. Independent scientists came to consider the early results unreliable. A very few samples did contain toxins: but both Canadian and British scientists later reported that, contrary to the US administration's contentions, the toxins could be made by moulds in the natural environment, and stored on cereals.

Questions still remained. If the samples were pollen excreted from bees, how could they fall like rain in concentrated showers? This puzzle was cleared up in 1984, during a visit to Southeast Asia by American scientists who were actually caught in a faecal shower: "We were visiting a region known for bee trees in which an unusually large number of nests are suspended. In the village of Khua Moong, about 24 kilometers south of Chiang Mai in Thailand, we examined the area around two such trees ... As we observed the second tree through binoculars from a clearing about 150 meters away, we saw a lightening in the color of several nests. Hundreds of thousands of bees were suddenly leaving their nests. Moments later drops of bee faeces began falling on and around the three members of our party. About a dozen spots fell on each of us. We could neither see nor hear the bees flying high above us ... the showers and spots closely resemble the showers and spots said to be caused by yellow rain."[37]

There was still some evidence dangling. What about the evidence given by the Hmong tribespeople? There were various forays to interview them, and it was not clear that all of their information was reliable. So in 1983 the US Defense and State

Departments sent a joint team of expert interviewers in to discover exactly what their evidence was. The team worked in Thailand for nearly two years, and discovered that there had been major flaws in both in previous selection of people for interviews and the interviews themselves. The people selected were only those who reported attacks of yellow rain. There was no distinction made between eye witness accounts and hearsay. Many of the tribespeople, when interviewed again, made it clear they had not themselves seen what they had spoken of. The dates originally specified by the Hmong—and which US intelligence had related to other events which, it said, backed up the BW attack theory—turned out to be the result of cultural confusion. The interviewers began to understand that the Hmong do not conceptualise time in the same way as Americans do. They do not think in terms of days or hours, but of seasons; and so the specific dates reported earlier were shown to be suspect.

The medical evidence presented by the Americans in 1981 with such conviction also began to evaporate. It had evidently been based on hearsay rather than medical examinations. When the expert interviewers were able to examine people who complained that they had been exposed to yellow rain, their symptoms were concluded to have resulted from a variety of other things: in one case, for example, "battle fatigue, smoke inhalation, heat stress or a combination of these effects."[38]

In spite of all the accumulated evidence, the US administration has never admitted that it was wrong. And its accusations fell on receptive ears amongst those who allocate funds for biological weapons research. During the 1980s, US support for BW research—along with all military activities during President Reagan's term of office—increased fourfold.

ISRAEL AND BW

"I met one of his commanders in a lecture in Jerusalem. I asked him whether my brother had really attempted to poison wells. 'These were the weapons we had', he said, 'and that's that.' "[39]

Rachel Katzman was trying to find out whether her brother, an Israeli soldier called David Horeen, had been sent on a military mission to poison Egyptian army wells in Gaza in 1948. He had set off with fellow soldier David Mizrahi in May, 1948, but they were quickly caught. Three months later both were hanged. Under interrogation, Horeen had admitted that he had been given a container of typhoid and dysentery bacteria to drop into the Egyptians' wells.

If this mission ended in failure, a similar one in the Arab town of Acre did not. It was captured on 17 May, 1948. By that time a typhoid epidemic was already raging there. According to military historian Uri Milstein, the army poisoned its water sources—as well as those of many Arab villages that were captured. It did not want their inhabitants to return.[40]

Israelis are particularly sensitive about allegations that they have used biological weapons. There are no official publications on the subject. These early attacks probably resulted from the work of HEMED B, the acronym for a military biological science corps that existed between 1948 and 1952. Brigadier Shlomo Gur, who headed the main HEMED organisation, claims to have been physically and emotionally removed from the work the biologists did: "I had no time to deal with the logistics of setting up the scientists' unit. I was busy manufacturing weapons in the workshops . . . The biologists got together quite spontaneously . . . I had an instinctive emotional sense that we did not need that."[41]

US intelligence sources believe that Israel has the capability to produce biological weapons but has not stockpiled them. The work is said to have been done at the highly fortified Biological Research Institute in Nes Ziona, ten miles south of Tel Aviv. That was where Professor Marcus Klingberg was deputy managing director before he was jailed for spying in 1983.

Klingberg, a Polish Jew whose family perished at Treblinka, escaped to the Soviet Union and graduated in medicine from the University of Minsk in 1941.[42] He joined the Soviet Medical Corps, where he was said to have solved the riddle of the deaths of thousands of civilians. They all lived in the Russian town of Orenburg, in a region which stored a lot of wheat. The deadly agent turned out to be a fungus that had grown in the wheat stores and which produced a powerful toxin, lethal in microscopic quantities. It has been reported that it was this toxin that the Soviets were meant to have used in "Yellow Rain." Presumably these reports may now be discounted, along with the existence of "Yellow Rain" itself.

Klingberg went to live in Israel in 1949. From the Medical Service he joined the Biological Institute. His job often took him abroad, and it was while his colleagues assumed he was on his way to a scientific meeting in Europe in 1983 that the Israelis secretly arrested, tried and jailed him for spying for the Soviet Union. No official information is available in Israel about the case. Some reports put his sentence at 18 years, others at 20.

Nobody knows what information he passed on, or how he may have helped the Soviet BW programme. But the severity of the sentence and the secrecy surrounding the case suggests that he must—by 1983 standards—have been a rich store of knowledge about biological weapons.

Now nearly 80, Klingberg is said to be terminally ill. The Israeli authorities finally released him in September 1998 to spend his last days quietly with his family.[43]

GERMAN BW DURING WORLD WAR I

Baron Otto Karl von Rosen, an aristocrat of Swedish/Finnish/German descent, was arrested with companions in Karasjok in Northeastern Norway in January 1917. The Baron was suspected of espionage and sabotage—he was carrying tins labelled "Swedish meat," which actually contained dynamite—and was briefly imprisoned before being extradited to Sweden. Only after the incident was over were other compromising articles found in his luggage, including nineteen sugar cubes, each containing a tiny glass tube filled with anthrax.

Norway was neutral during the First World War, but allowed British arms to be transported across its northern wastes by horses and reindeer to the Russians, to help them fight the Germans. The Baron, who was working for the Germans, was to feed the sugar lumps to the animals to infect them with a probably lethal dose of anthrax.

The Norwegian affair was part of a larger German attempt to target animals supplied to its enemies by neutral trading partners. According to Mark Wheelis at the University of California, German agents were sent to at least five countries—Rumania, Spain, Norway, the US and Argentina—with "microbial cultures and instructions to infect shipments to the Allies of horses, mules, cattle and sheep. The bacteria used were those that cause anthrax and glanders." Until about mid-1916, agents targeted horses and mules shipped to the Allies from the eastern coast of the US. "A crew of longshoremen recruited by the Germans wandered among the stockades where animals were collected for trans-shipment, jabbing them with needles dipped into the microbial cultures," writes Wheelis. The Germans also targeted Rumanian animals being supplied to Russia (co-opting Bulgarian agents for the purpose); and more anthrax-loaded sugar cubes were prepared for Spanish horses being shipped to France, and cattle, horses and mules supplied by Argentina to the Allies.

It is not known how many animals were killed. Anthrax is not contagious, so the animals would not have passed it on to each other. What has emerged, however, is just how long anthrax can last. Two sugar cubes with their ampoules were found by the curator of a police museum in Trondheim, Norway, in 1998, and ended up being analyzed at Porton Down. Using special techniques, scientists there were able to "revive a few surviving organisms from the brink of extinction after they had been stored, without any special precautions, for 80 years."

SOUTH AFRICA'S BW MASTERMIND

In February 1997, Dr Wouter Basson was hauled alive out of a pond in a Pretoria park by a police hit squad. He had fled from his house when it was raided following a sting operation initiated by the CIA. The Americans wanted to "contain" Basson, who was planning to leave South Africa with his secret archives on the chemical and biological weapons programme he had headed during the apartheid era. When his travel plans became known to the CIA, that organisation reportedly tipped off the Pretoria authorities that he had a large quantity of ecstasy tablets. The authorities pounced. Basson fled to the pond. He was later arrested.

At his bail hearing, Mike Kennedy, the National Intelligence Agency's chief director for counter intelligence organisations, was allowed to give evidence in camera but a judge later ordered that his statement could be reported by the press. Kennedy had argued that Basson was wanted by foreign intelligence organisations because of his knowledge of chemical and biological warfare, and that it would be dangerous to release him. "There are a number of intelligence services which have given very clear indications that it would not be safe for Dr Basson to travel overseas," Kennedy explained, adding: "it would be detrimental to his health."

The NIA director told the court that some former Eastern bloc countries "have the ability to wipe out half to three-quarters of the world with diseases." Contrary to official denials, South Africa's programme in the 1980s had been for offensive and not merely defensive purposes. Kennedy said that after Basson had retired, in 1993, and when the ANC led by Nelson Mandela was poised to win control, "vast measures" had been put in place to keep the extent of South Africa's earlier chemical and biological warfare programme secret.

Basson's trial, on charges of murder, theft, fraud and possession of large quantities of ecstasy and mandrax tablets, began in August 1998.

7

SCIENTIFIC DEVELOPMENTS AND BW

Scientific developments are increasing the threat of biological warfare. This chapter outlines those developments in more detail, beginning with a look back to our earliest use of micro-organisms for food and pleasure.

BEER, BREAD AND BUGS

The Sumerians and Babylonians enjoyed beer as long ago as 6000 B.C.E. It is not known whether they learned about the delights of beer or bread first, but both are made by manipulating living organisms. Take bread, for example: a mixture of flour, yeast, sugar and salt. What makes it rise is carbon dioxide, given off by the reaction between the living yeast cells and the sugar in a process called fermentation. The same process is crucial for beer-making too, in which barley and yeast ferment. Living organisms are also used in baking, and to produce cheese, yogurt, wine and oriental foods such as soy sauce and tempeh.

Because the action of micro-organisms is crucial to the making of these foods, their manufacture comes under the heading of biotechnology: "the use of living organisms and their components in agriculture, food and other industrial processes."[1] Modern biotechnology encompasses antibiotics and vaccines, new crop varieties, pesticides and fertilisers. All of these are made using living organisms. Biotechnological processes also allow us to treat sewage, diagnose disease and produce energy.

The essence of biotechnology is growing large numbers of cells under controlled conditions. As John E. Smith, Professor of Applied

Microbiology at Strathclyde University, describes it: "In its simplest form, the bioprocess can be seen as just mixing micro-organisms with a nutrient broth and allowing the components to react, eg yeast cells with a sugar solution to give alcohol."[2] The mixing and reaction take place in fermenters, and the product is then separated out and purified. This is essentially how all biotechnological products are made, whether alcohol, vaccines, cheese, antibiotics, animal feedstuffs or whatever. But just as micro-organisms are the basic components of beneficial biological products, so are they also the basis of biological war. Viruses processed to make vaccines can just as easily be produced for biological weapons. This so-called "dual-use" problem—that exactly the same technology can be used for both legitimate biotechnology and illegal weaponry—is one of the most difficult faced by negotiators trying to control the spread of biological weapons. We will return to this in Chapter 9. It means that, given the world-wide spread of biotechnology, at least one hundred countries have the technological capability to produce biological weapons. And this is not the only problem. The nature of modern biotechnological equipment makes it easier for countries who want to misuse it.

Biotechnology plants used to be identified by large stainless steel or glass fermenters, commonly holding up to 10,000 liters. But, as with all technologies, components have become smaller: about a thousand times smaller for computer-controlled, continuous-flow fermenters. "As a result of these improvements in production technology," writes Jonathan Tucker of the US Arms Control and Disarmament Agency, "the manufacture of BW agents and toxins could take place in small, insconspicuous facilities without the need for a full-scale plant, blurring the former distinction between a laboratory and a production facility."[3] Thus, clandestine production of agents for biological weapons becomes ever easier. "Moreover," continues Tucker, "since pathogenic [i.e. disease-causing] bacteria can be grown from a few organisms to a ton of agent in a period of days or weeks, the time needed to acquire a militarily significant stockpile has greatly diminished."[4]

These developments in biotechnology are part of the reason we should be taking the biological weapons threat seriously. There is another, however, which could have even worse consequences;

and that is scientists' newly found ability to design and create more effective agents. To see how this has come about, we need to fill in a bit of biological background.

HER MOTHER'S NOSE?

Long before scientists understood the structure of our genes, people had realized that the nature of animals and plants is largely influenced by their parents. For centuries, we have tried to create the animals and plants we want by breeding them from parents whose characteristics we want to reproduce. Crossing them to make new types was the first genetic manipulation humans engaged in, and it has produced tremendous variety: think, for example, of the different shapes and sizes of all the breeds of domestic dogs.

Working like this, however, at the level of the whole organism, is a random process which takes a long time, is unpredictable and sometimes does not work at all. The playwright George Bernard Shaw understood this. He was once asked by a beautiful woman whether they shouldn't have a child together: with her beauty and his brains, she said, they would produce a remarkable person. To which he replied, "Yes, madam, but what if the child should have my beauty and your brains?"

During the last 20 years or so, plant breeders have developed a more controlled way of breeding flowers, using cells of plants rather than the whole organism.

It produces more predictable results, much faster, and enables plants to be produced in climates where they could not normally grow.

It is now possible, however, to manipulate living organisms even more precisely: at the level of the genes themselves.

THE STUFF OF LIFE

In 1953, James Watson and Francis Crick elucidated the structure of the chemical DNA (deoxyribose nucleic acid), which makes up our genes. It was a momentous discovery which has given rise to modern biotechnology and genetic engineering. Genes carry our biological heritage. When sperm meets egg, a new genetic individual is created. Each human parent donates one set of 23 chromosomes, which look like tiny rods, to the new cell. The chromosomes carry the DNA, which is made up of four sub-units of chemicals, known by their first letters as A, T, G and C. These are the letters that spell out the words—the genes—that make up the recipes that make us. The genetic code of each human being is three billion letters long.

The structure of DNA—the famous double helix, or twisted ladder—is crucial for its replication and thus the sustaining of life. But it is not only reproduction that this arrangement makes possible. Using an essential intermediary called ribose nucleic acid or RNA, the DNA also directs the design and assembly of proteins, which are necessary for maintaining life. There are millions of different proteins, and they form the structures of our cells. They are part of the thousands of chemical and physical reactions that our bodies need to perform to remain alive. They also protect us from disease.

Our bodies are the result of the recipe set out for our proteins by our genes. John E. Smith uses a different analogy: "Genes," he says, "may be viewed as the biological software and are the programs that drive the growth, development and functioning of an organism."[5] Want to know whether someone is male or female?—or what color her eyes are?—or whether he will suffer from Huntington's disease? The genes will tell you.

This is not to say, of course, that our genes determine all aspects of our lives. One of the most vociferous debates today is about the extent to which our genes do influence us—our general health, personalities, sexual preferences and so on. So far, research suggests that we are probably equally influenced by the experiences we have and the environments we live in. One thing is certain, though: understanding how specific genes are constructed will teach us a tremendous amount about how our bodies function.

DNA makes up not only our genes but also the genes of every other living thing on the planet, whether tree, flower, pig, beetle, fish—or bacterium. When we examine the DNA of any live organisms, we are looking at them in the same terms.

Even viruses, which are parasites and need to colonise another organism before they can replicate; even these simplest forms of almost-life are made up of DNA or RNA. Not as much as we have—in fact, less than one-millionth as much—but, nevertheless, they are made of the same stuff as we are. And the way they work is laid down by their genetic material. Want to know what makes some viruses virulent and others not? Why some are transmissible in blood and others through the atmosphere? Why some are hard to catch and others easy? It's their genes that make them that way.

POWERFUL KNOWLEDGE

As our knowledge of our genes deepens, we will gain an ever-more-detailed comprehension of the way our bodies work. We will be able to understand how specific molecules—at the most fundamental physical and chemical level of life—interact. We will also see how they can be disrupted—and, as we learn to mend the damage, we will open the way to advances in medicine. These will come through being able to manipulate genes: to repair them when they are faulty, so that they carry out their functions properly. And our knowledge of our genetic structure is growing all the time, especially through the Human Genome Project. This is the largest international government-sponsored project in the life sciences: to elucidate the entire genetic structure of a human being. Current progress suggests that this enormous task will be achieved by about 2003. The aim of this project is laudable: "to provide insight into the organisation and function of genetic material and in the course of this work to base physiology and medicine on solid molecular foundations, to provide the chemical basis for understanding hereditary diseases, and to aid understanding of the mechanisms of immune response and the appearance of cancerous tumors."[6]

But this same knowledge will also give us a greater understanding of how we can attack the body; and we will be able to manipulate genes to that end as well. We will be able to change viruses and bacteria to make new forms which would be more suitable for biological weapons.

In theory, anything is possible. According to Jeffrey Almond, Professor in the School of Animal and Microbial Sciences at the University of Reading, "it has become apparent that the possibilities for constructing new and potentially sinister versions of micro-organisms . . . are almost limitless."[7] Take, for example, viruses which cause influenza.

LETHAL FLU

Not only people get flu: so do other animals. In general, the flu viruses which infect humans do not kill us, even though they make us feel dreadful. The Spanish flu epidemic which swept the world in 1918 and 1919, and is estimated to have killed about 20 million people, was an exception. There are flu viruses which infect birds, however, which kill more than 90 percent of the birds that become ill. Clearly these are very virulent organisms. Scientists have now discovered which genes cause this virulence—although they do not yet know how they do it. They now understand the genetic mixture which make some flu viruses so virulent that they kill nearly all their avian victims, whereas others are so mild that the infected birds hardly know there is anything wrong. But scientists have gone further than theoretical understanding. Japanese scientists Horimoto and Kawaoka, from the Graduate School of Veterinary Medicine in Hokkaido, have proved they are right, by changing the genetic structure of a virulent turkey virus and making it into one that causes much less severe disease.[8] The genetic difference between the two viruses is subtle; but the effect of the difference is enormous. In this case the virus was changed from virulent to benign, but it could also be engineered the other way.

If scientists can change a bird flu virus from a benign type to a highly virulent one, why can't they do the same for human flu viruses? Technically, they could. They have not done so: the legislation of most countries would prohibit it. No legitimate laboratory would touch it. But terrorists are not legitimate. And given the explosion in the skills and equipment needed for genetic engineering, the prerequisites are already available. Genetic engineering, this most modern form of biotechnology, is widely used in research in the pharmaceutical industry, the food industry and modern agriculture, as well as in microbiological laboratories. As Professor Almond says: "It should be pointed out that no special equipment is required for this technology; any modern, molecular biology laboratory would have the means to put it into practice. Modified influenza viruses resulting from such manipulations could readily be propagated in a standard laboratory. Influenza virus grows rapidly and well in embryonated hen eggs and yields from a single egg can be of the order of 10 ml of fluid which may have a [concentration] of a hundred million to a billion viruses per ml." In theory, one hen's egg would provide enough virus to infect everyone in the world twice over.[9] "These viruses spread rapidly by the respiratory route and would be highly infectious in aerosols" adds Professor Almond—and continues, chillingly, "The scale of operations would also seem to fall within the potential of terrorist groups . . . establishing the technology for the development of biological weapons is cheap and relatively simple and the skills are widespread."[10]

OTHER OPTIONS

There are many other ways in which biological warfare agents could be made more suitable as weapons. They could be modified so that, when weaponized in an aerosol, they would no longer be destroyed by light (that is, the sun's radiation). Dr Richard Novick, Director of the Public Health Research Institute of New York, writing with science journalist Seth Shulman, warns: "Certain bacteria are highly resistant to radiation and this resistance is due to a relatively small number of genes. These genes could readily be transplanted into a radiation-sensitive pathogenic organism with the intention of improving its ability to survive the radiation it would receive when aerosolised."[11] In the same way, it could be possible to engineer out other agents' susceptibility to desiccation.

Genetic engineering might also be able to shorten the incubation period of some agents from days to hours so that they would incapacitate the enemy more quickly. This would reduce some of the uncertainty associated with their use. Bacteria might also be engineered to include "conditional suicide genes," so that they would die after a certain time or if their environment were to change beyond a narrow range. This could help overcome the problem of agent infecting people downwind of the attack.

TOXINS AND OTHER SURPRISES

Fifteen years ago, toxins had to be extracted laboriously from large quantities of whatever they were made by. For example: 270 kilograms of clam siphons yielded less than 5 grams of the paralysing poison saxitoxin. These days, the gene that directs the production of the toxin can be isolated and inserted into bacteria that can be grown in fermenters, producing large amounts of toxin quickly. Or the toxin gene could be directly engineered into antibiotic-resistant bacteria that readily colonizes the human gut or respiratory tract, producing a new and deadly bacterium which would not be knocked out by known antibiotics. The same could be done into a virus. (Scorpion toxin has successfully been engineered into a virus that attacks caterpillars, to make a deadly pesticide.)

Some toxins, such as botulin and ricin, deteriorate rapidly when they are exposed to sunlight and oxygen and would be hard to use to their full effect in an aerosol. Just as in the case of the agents described above, however, genetic engineering could change them to overcome these disadvantages.

There is another group of naturally occurring substances ("bioregulators") that could be mass produced by genetic engineering to be used as biological weapons. These are a particular type of proteins usually present in minute quantities in our bodies that regulate body temperature, hormone release, mood, consciousness, sleep and emotions. If the regulating system gets out of balance by even a small amount, we suffer fear, pain, fatigue, depression, hallucinations—or go to sleep. It is unclear how these substances would be delivered, but they could in theory disorient people or animals and affect plants as well.

VIRUSES IN DEMAND

Up to the end of the 1960s, scientists had shown most interest in using bacterial or fungal agents for weapons. With the advent of genetic engineering in the seventies, however, attention turned to viruses. The new techniques enable some viruses, previously thought too dangerous to handle, to be manipulated more safely. Viruses have some advantages for use in biological weapons because the diseases they cause often have the same symptoms and are therefore hard to diagnose. They are also harder to treat than bacterial diseases, which can be fought with antibiotics.

Another reason for the suitability of viruses is that many vaccines are produced against viral diseases. This means that if a virus were modified—say the human influenza virus, to make it more virulent—then a vaccine could be produced that would protect against that particular new form. If one group of people were going to use the new virus against another, they could vaccinate their own troops against it so that they would be protected. Only the enemy would succumb. Biological warfare agents could also be slightly altered to bypass our bodies' usual defences. This happens all the time, as part of the natural progression of things. We go on catching colds and flu year after year, because the bug changes slightly over time, making our previous defence much weaker. Alternatively, an agent could be engineered to make it resistant to therapeutic drugs, so that the usual medical treatments against it would not work.

BACTERIA ARE BACK

It is a measure of the tremendous activity in genetic engineering that bacteria are now coming back onto the scientific—and therefore possibly the warfare—agenda. Unlike viruses, bacteria are free-living, and their genetic material therefore contains all the information necessary to sustain life. In July, 1995, the prestigious American journal *Science* carried a report of the first unravelling of the entire genetic structure of a bacterium called *H. influenzae*. It is "a benign laboratory strain [i.e., type] of a bacterium that in its wild form can cause ear infections and meningitis."[12]

The report summarises some of the implications of the work, which "is destined to change the tranquil backwaters of microbiology into a surging torrent of new discoveries: . . . helping to identify genes that transform harmless bacteria into killers . . . Comparing the genomes of virulent and harmless strains of bacteria will further aid microbiologists in their search for disease-causing genes." These advances are welcomed for the progress they will allow scientists to make in understanding and combating disease. One example cited by the report concerns how bacteria spread in sneezes. The genetic structure of *H. influenzae* seems to be especially adapted to allow this to happen. It is fascinating: a breathtaking glimpse into the nitty-gritty of the way this organism has evolved to exploit its environment; a microbiological demonstration of Darwin's theory of evolution. It is expanding and deepening our knowledge of the way we are made. It will also reveal to us more about how we can be un-made, and therefore adds to the increasing potential for misuse.

The implications for biological warfare also flow from the way the work was carried out. The scientists involved were using a new tech-nique that they had invented: computer programmes which speed up the elucidation of the genetic structure of the organism, and en-able it to be done far more cheaply than before. As the leader of the scientific team, Professor Craig Venter, pointed out: "People thought [that bacterial] were mulitiyear, multimillion-dollar projects. We've shown that it can be done in less than a year and [remarkably cheaply]." And because so much of the work is done on the com-puter, says David Smith, the Director of the Department of Energy's genome project, "it's going to empower the small investigator in ways that they had never dreamt." It's a milestone for science. It's also a big step in the right direction for terrorists. As in traditional biotechnology, the equipment needed for elucidating genetic struc-tures is becoming smaller and cheaper and more available.

At the moment, most experts agree, reliable genetic engineering of micro-organisms could not be guaranteed. A virus whose infec-tivity is boosted, for example, may have its virulence lessened. Not enough is yet known about the interactions between various prop-erties of micro-organisms to make sure that one which has been en-gineered for a particular effect will work as predicted. But it is only a matter of time. In theory, genetic engineering could also be used to make entirely new micro-organisms that could be used as bio-logical weapons. In practice, many are sceptical that this would work. The disease-causing properties of bacteria and viruses are complex and not wholly understood; and it seems unlikely at the moment that an artificially created organism—one made by trying to produce a hybrid of two nasty bacteria, for example—would be more dangerous than many already found in nature.

ETHNIC WEAPONS

There is another horrifying possibility of genetic engineering: a weapon made to attack a specific ethnic group. Thus, it has been suggested, a mixture of influenza or diphtheria could be designed to affect mainly blacks; a "designer toxin" could be aimed exclusively at Serbs; or people with blue eyes might be given Alzheimer's disease. The US Navy thought of this as long ago as 1951—way before the advent of genetic engineering—presumably on the basis of the observation that Negroes are much more likely than whites to die from valley fever, a disease caught from a fungus endemic in California's San Joaquin Valley. The Navy carried out a trial at one of its supply depots in Pennsylvania, using a benign organism to mimic valley fever fungus. The ostensible reason for the trial was that, as many Negroes worked at the depot, its operation would be severely affected if they were incapacitated.

Sober and respected voices have begun to sound alarm bells about this possibility. A recent Yearbook from the Stockholm International Peace Research Institute warns that genetic differences so far found "may in many cases be sufficiently large and stable so as to possibly be exploited by using naturally occurring, selective agents or by genetically engineering organisms and toxins..."[13] The former head of Sweden's Defence Research Establishment, General Bo Rybeck, voiced similar fears at a meeting of the International Committee of the Red Cross early in 1996. Genetic weapons, he says, may be "just around the corner."[14] Also in 1996, the World Medical Congress in South Africa was warned about the danger of ethnic weapons. Dr Vivienne Nathanson, head of science and ethics for the British Medical Association, told the congress: "One could imagine in Rwanda, a weapon which targeted one of the two tribal groups, the Tutsi and Hutu. While these weapons do not, so far as we know, exist, it is not very far away scientifically." And in 1997, US Defense Secretary Cohen was quoted as saying that "the scientific community is 'very close' to being able to manufacture 'genetically engineered pathogens that could be ethnically specific.' "[15]

How close are we, scientifically, to being able to develop such weapons? The British Medical Association considers this question in a major report it published in January, 1999 ("Biotechnology, weapons and humanity"). The very fact that the BMA is concerned enough about the possibility to produce the report is significant in itself. Biological weapons, and their genetic offspring, are no longer the preserve of international negotiators. Doctors should act, according to the report, "to protect the integrity of their work."

The crux of the science that is ushering in the age of genetic weapons is the Human Genome Project, which we have already described. By about 2003, it is expected to have sequenced the entire human genome. This work will lead to intensive research on how the genome works. It was therefore no surprise that, in January 1999, the British government allocated the UK Biotechnology and Biological Sciences Research Council £15 million for research on "genomics": in the Council's words, "the new science and technology that allows information about the DNA sequences of genes to be translated into an understanding of their function and behaviour." As we have already said, understanding how our genes work will enable us to interfere with how they work, for good and ill.

Genetic difference between groups

In order to target a specific ethnic population, we have to know which genes differentiate them from others. It is true that races are social and cultural categories, not genetic ones; and it is also true that there is far more genetic diversity within any one population than between different populations. Nevertheless, there are differences in the frequency with which any particular form of a gene is found in a group of people. Each of our genes can occur in different forms ("alleles," as they are known by geneticists). Thus we all have a blood type—A, B or O—but which type any one person has is determined by the particular form of the gene. And some populations have more A's, B's or O's than others. The pattern of variation between individuals differs from group to group, and the extremes of this variation mark one group off from another.

This sort of delineation would not however be neat and tidy. A weapon which targeted the most common form of a gene in a certain population would not wipe it out totally, and the effects of the weapon would not be confined only to that group. Neither do populations fit neatly into geographical or political boundaries. Anyone contemplating the use of such weapons would have to be prepared to kill part of his own as well as other friendly populations. Scrupulousness, however, is not likely to be foremost in the character of anyone who would be prepared to unleash genetic warfare.

According to the BMA report, there are two scientific efforts apart from the Human Genome Project which are crucial to the development of genetic weapons. In recent years, genetic differences between groups have been studied by the Human Genome Diversity Project, which collects genetic material from 500 isolated and endangered populations from round the world for research on human history and biology. It is already reported to have discovered hundreds of parts of the genome which differ between populations. DNA fingerprinting, so widely used in court to nail criminals on the basis of their genetic make-up, works by estimating the probability that the particular gene sequence found at the scene of the crime comes from the suspect. This sort of work may also make it possible to identify sequences found more frequently in some groups than in others.

Work on the genetic differences between groups is proceeding. In 1997, a group of researchers (Shriver et al) reported in the *American Journal of Human Genetics* that they had been able, on the basis of genetic analysis, to predict whether people were African Americans, European Americans or Hispanic Americans.[16] They said they would be able to develop similar methods of identifying other populations common in the United States.

Thus, the Human Genome Project and the Human Genome Diversity Project are uncovering our genetic structures and how they differ between groups. The BMA report enumerates a third development, however, which will enable us to tinker with these differences. And that is gene therapy.

Gene therapy

Researchers in medical genetics are conducting work which will revolutionise cures for some diseases. They are tracking down the genetic malfunctions that result in illness. They already know that a fault in a single gene causes, for example, cystic fibrosis, some colorectal cancer, Huntington's disease, early onset breast cancer, early onset Alzheimer's, Tay-Sachs disease (which is one thousand times more common amongst Ashkenazi Jews than the rest of the population), muscular dystrophy and haemophilia. Diseases caused by a single gene are relatively rare, however. People become susceptible to most common diseases (cancers, diabetes, heart disease, high blood pressure, stroke and mental illnesses such as schizophrenia and manic depression) by having several faulty genes and by the influence on them of lifestyle and environmental factors.

The long-term aim of this research is to devise ways of manipulating the faulty genes so that they work properly, and the patient is cured. In order to do this, a corrective mechanism has to be introduced into the cells in which the defective gene is expressed. There are various ways in which this is being tried.[17] One is to load a "vector"—a carrier—(often, a particular sort of virus) with DNA that will correct the fault, and integrate it back into the patient's genes. Trials for cystic fibrosis patients are using these principles to give relief from the disease. Another method is to introduce a toxic payload into, say, cancer cells, to destroy them. There are problems in making sure that the inserted material only goes to the affected cells and that it continues to do its job there; but these and other sorts of gene therapies depend on being able to target particular gene sequences inside affected cells. They are very powerful techniques. And, because of the tremendous benefits they are likely to convey, they are being intensively researched.

It does not take much imagination to see how these developments could be misused. Instead of manipulating genes for good, the unscrupulous could target sequences unusual for their frequency in a certain group of people, and could change them to cause disease and death.

Such weapons would be particularly detestable. But the 1990s war in former Yugoslavia, with its ethnic cleansing, or the genocide of the 1994 war in Rwanda, should leave nobody in any doubt of the hatreds that can still exist between different populations. The possibility, however remote, that ethnic weapons could be made shows the urgency of reinforcing international condemnation of all forms of biological warfare.

ANIMALS AND PLANTS

This chapter has so far dealt with agents—natural or modified—that could be used to attack people. Exactly the same principles apply to those that could be targeted at plants or animals.

Pests that eat crops could be genetically engineered to be resistant to common pesticides. The result could be similar to what happened in the Imperial Valley in south-east California in 1991, when a new strain of whitefly caused a $300–million loss in agricultural earnings. The outbreak was not assumed to be a BW attack but rather a naturally evolved resistant strain. If an aggressor were to modify a pest already endemic to the region that was to be attacked, there would be fewer suspicions of foul play. Pests could also be engineered to eat a specific crop—one that the enemy depended on for economic survival.

Biotechnology has been put to work for crops. Selective breeding produced the so-called Green Revolution of the 1960s, with its higher-yielding varieties of maize, wheat and rice in some Third World countries. They replaced the many different strains that farmers had bred to suit local conditions; thus they reduced the genetic diversity of staple crops. The same trend is apparent in developed countries, too. One study shows that over 90 percent of commercially available varieties of US vegetable crops have disappeared since the turn of the century.[18] Widespread reliance on only a few varieties—as few as five or six in any particular country—means that any pest or disease that attacks them can wreak havoc and wipe out a huge fraction of any crop. And of course similar damage would be caused by an engineered agent against which they had no resistance.

HOW SOON?

It is generally agreed that nations wanting to develop clandestine BW programmes would, at the moment, concentrate on traditional agents like anthrax and botulinum toxin: ones that are well known and well understood. They could be easily and quickly produced in modern biotechnological plants, without the need for genetic engineering. What of the more sophisticated genetic engineering techniques?—how plausible is it that they will soon be used in connection with biological weapons?

In 1994, Malcolm Dando, Professor of International Security at the University of Bradford, and an expert on BW, gave a sober assessment: "Maybe for the next decade [genetic engineering capabilities] will remain predominantly in the hands of Western countries, but it seems to be unlikely 20 years from now. Certainly in 50 years' time, the ability to construct many different kinds of new biological weaponry will surely be widespread. What today would require the ingenuity of a Nobel Prize-winner will by then be commonplace."[19] It is a measure of the pace of research in this area that, in 1999, Dr Vivienne Nathanson of the British Medical Association predicted that the technology would be available to make genetic weapons within ten years.

Unfortunately, the "Western countries" that Professor Dando was referring to may have to include Western terrorists. It is reported that the Japanese sect Aum Shin Rikyo took delivery from US companies of "sophisticated molecular design software," whose purpose is "to re-engineer the molecular structure of chemicals or micro-organisms to make them stronger or more dangerous."[20] The bellicose fruits of the biotechnology revolution may ripen and fall faster than we think.

RUSSIAN GENETICALLY ENGINEERED AGENTS

In April 1997, it was reported by the publication "Jane's Land-based Air Defence" that the Russian Federation has developed a new, genetically-engineered variant of anthrax that is totally resistant to antibiotics. The information had come from defectors and Western intelligence sources, and the editors called it "the final Doomsday Scenario."

The new variant was developed by the quasi-civilian organisation Biopreparat, now known to be a cover for the Russian biological warfare programme.

The editors chillingly commented: "It only needs this to be independently discovered by an ostracised nation's scientists, and then developed for missile delivery, for an Armageddon situation to occur whereby the only reliable retribution may be overwhelming nuclear response."

With the upheavals in Russia following the collapse of Communism, many fear that some Russian scientists might sell their expertise to the highest bidder. Information about how to make biological weapons is in any case no longer secret. It is freely available on the Internet.

8

DEFENSE AGAINST BIOLOGICAL WARFARE

During the 1991 Gulf War, the Israelis expected Iraq to attack them with chemical or biological warheads. They were issued with gas masks and given instructions about preparing a sealed room with essential provisions—bottled drinking water, flashlights, candles and matches, canned foods, etc. Anxiety, already high, became acute when the first air-raid sirens woke the population at 2 A.M. on 18 January. In spite of official predictions that several hours' warning would be given, the first Scud missile fell just two minutes later. On that day, eight missiles landed in and around Tel Aviv and Haifa.

The Israelis' experiences waiting for chemical and biological attack resonate with human reactions: the mother who was stunned that part of her newly-born son's layette was a plastic-covered crib with a filtered ventilator to protect him against nerve gas and anthrax; the four-year old girl who created a sealed room in her dolls' house for her dolls; the T-shirts depicting primates at various stages of evolution, the last one a human wearing a gas mask, and a caption saying "What went wrong?." Protection brought its own tragedy. A three-year old girl was suffocated in a struggle with her parents who were trying to put her gas mask on.[1]

The attacks also produced a novelty: a paper in the medical journal *The Lancet* by five doctors from the Kaplan Hospital in Rehovot who delivered babies while under fire. As soon as the sirens sounded, the midwives, obstetricians, pediatricians, paramedical personnel and patients put on gas masks: "To the best of our knowledge, labour and delivery while wearing a gas mask has not been described previously."[2] The babies did not appear to be affected.

In the event, the Iraqis did not use chemical or biological warheads. The Israelis' experience showed that the public was not roused to organize defence until the threat was imminent, and that confusion about proper defensive measures continued throughout the war. This in a country which already had extensive shelters for civil defence—unlike, for example, the UK—and where everyone was issued with a gas mask.

In the UK, the Home Office is responsible for overall planning for civil emergencies, but operational control rests with local authorities' fire, ambulance and police services.[3] There is no specific guidance at local level about protection from a BW attack. Local authorities would look to Ministry of Defence scientific advisors for information about the type and nature of the BW agent.

According to Dr Graham Pearson, former Director of the UK's biological defence establishment at Porton Down, defence programmes need to consider both military and civilian populations; and "[t]he possibilities for defence of the civilian population need to be debated to a greater extent than they have been."[4] What measures could reasonably be taken to protect the population from BW attack?

IS DEFENSE POSSIBLE?

Crops

Plants do not have an immune system, and so are more vulnerable to biological agents than people are. The only way to protect crops against biological agents would be to plant types that were resistant to them or to make sure a suitable pesticide was available. In practice this would mean knowing in advance what agent would be used. Intelligence cannot be dismissed out of hand, but this knowledge may only be available to the aggressor.

Food poisoning

"I got up out of bed feeling sick. Eventually I was violently sick. I hadn't the strength to go into the toilet. I ended up lying on the sofa with a towel wrapped round me like a baby's nappy . . ." This is how Mary Cairns described what it was like to have food poisoning from *E.Coli* 0157.[5] Her kidneys and bowels failed; she survived only after kidney dialysis and intensive care in hospital. She was one of four hundred people affected in the worst-ever outbreak of food poisoning in the UK, in Scotland in November, 1996. It was caused by *E.Coli* 0157 in gravy in meat pies supplied by a butcher in Wishaw.

Eighteen people died in the outbreak. There is no suggestion whatever that this was a BW event; but when people fall ill there is no immediate way of knowing whether the cause is accidental or deliberate. It is fair to assume that the authorities would not have reacted any differently to begin with even if they had realised, later on, that the outbreak had been a BW attack.

When a patient goes to a doctor with food poisoning, the doctor tries to guess what bacterium is causing the problem on the basis of the patient's symptoms and story. Then there is a delay while the micro-organism is sent to the Public Health Laboratory Service in London for further analysis. The standard microbiological tests take about 48 hours to give a result. They involve mushing up some of the suspected food, allowing the bacteria in it to grow and then identifying them. The process needs to be done slowly and carefully when, as in the case of *E. Coli* 0157, only about ten of the organisms are enough to cause infection and there may be thousands of other bacteria present in the sample. The turnaround time lengthens the process still more, especially in the summer when most of the incidents occur. This identifies the strain of organism but not its unique molecular structure.

There are other, quicker ways of discovering what contaminants are. Gene probes, which identify micro-organisms at the molecular level, give results in two or three hours. But this degree of analysis is not routinely used to identify an agent which has caused a threat to public health. In those cases, linking all the sick people with a particular source, and identifying the strain of bacteria from that source, is usually enough. There is no need for the precision that molecular analysis gives. "We only go to the molecular level when we absolutely categorically need to nail it," says Christine Murphy of the Public Health Laboratory Service at Collindale in London.[6]

The identification of the micro-organism is not the only thing that takes time. In the Scottish case, it took the authorities five days to release a list of other outlets supplied by the butcher at the centre of the outbreak. This delay was because they did not want to jeop-ardise the businesses of the other outlets before they were certain that they had received products from the original butcher's. The list the authorities first supplied contained about 50 outlets, but these grew as time went on. In the meantime, people ate products from the secondary suppliers, and became ill.

Food poisoning agents that would be likely to be used in a BW attack—botulinum, eg—act more quickly than *E. Coli* 0157, whose incubation period is about three to four days. If the authorities took the same time to warn of possible secondary outlets, casualties in a BW scenario would be far higher than in the *E.Coli* outbreak. Add to this the probability that any attacker would infect food with a large dose of agent, to make sure of a dramatic effect, and the casu-alties would be even higher again.

Medical countermeasures

In theory, the effects of many BW agents could be countered by vaccination before exposure, to build up resistance to viral agents. After exposure, antibiotics could be used against bacteria.

Vaccination would involve many problems. There are no vac-cines for humans against some potential BW agents: brucellosis, for example (although antibiotics are generally effective against bru-cellosis). Vaccines against other agents are in different stages of de-velopment and efficacy in different countries. The anthrax vaccine being used to immunise the entire US military force—an immu-nization programme expected to last until 2003—has the confi-dence of the Pentagon. Dr Sue Bailey, Assistant Secretary of Defense for Health Affairs, said at a press briefing on 14 August 1998 that "This vaccine is thought at this point to be effective against all the strains [of anthrax] we know about . . ." However Victor Sidal, professor of Social Medicine at Yeshiva University in New York, quotes contradictory results from trials of the vaccine in guinea pigs and monkeys and concludes that "[T]here is no good reason to believe that the . . . vaccine will be effective in protecting troops against airborne infection with anthrax . . ." He also refers to the Senate Veterans Affairs Committee which examined the effi-cacy and safety of the vaccine in 1995, and which recommended that "the vaccine should be considered investigational when used as a protection against biologic warfare." Professor Sidal also raises questions about the vaccine's safety.

Vaccination will be ineffective against strains of anthrax that have been genetically engineered to overcome the current vaccine. Russian researchers reported in 1997 that they had developed a new strain of anthrax, and the Russian defector Dr Ken Alibeck, previously the first deputy chief of research and production for the Soviet biological weapons programme, has asserted that the USSR had genetically engineered strains of anthrax to circumvent current vaccines.

Even where vaccines do exist they may not be effective against disease agents introduced in the unnatural way that BW would involve: the current plague vaccine is, for example, believed to be effective against bubonic plague (passed on in flea bites) but not against aerosolised and inhaled plague bacteria. And given that BW would expose people to far larger doses of micro-organisms than usual, vaccines may be overwhelmed.

It would also be hard to know what to vaccinate against. To overcome this problem, scientists are developing vaccines designed to protect against several diseases at once; however these can produce problems if they interact in unexpected ways, as they seem to have done in military personnel involved in the Gulf War (see box, Chapter 4).

In practice, it would only be military personnel who would be immunised against BW agents. According to Colonel David Franz, former Director of the US Army Medical Research Institute of Infectious Diseases at Fort Detrick, "[F]or civilian populations, pre-exposure medical countermeasures would likely not be used."

What, then, of medical help for civilians who have been subjected to a BW attack? There are many problems with antibiotics and other post-exposure medications such as antitoxins and antidotes. Such drugs are best given as soon after exposure as possible; but how will Governments know that an attack has taken place except when people fall ill? "The unfortunate fact remains," writes Colonel Franz, "that humans are often the most sensitive, or the only, detector of a biological attack."

Some diseases are untreatable by the time they have progressed far enough to show symptoms. To be effective, antibiotics would have to be administered within about six hours of an attack—which, given the time usually taken to identify micro-organisms, would be impossible. Diagnosis would be difficult because hardly any General Practitioners in developed countries are familiar with BW agents and the symptoms they cause. It would be made even more difficult if more than one agent were used; and what to do if the drug necessary for one disease was incompatible with that needed for another? The massive doses of BW agent may well be too much for ordinary antibiotic or antitoxin regimes. And the huge numbers of people involved would probably overwhelm all diagnostic and treatment facilities. During the Gulf War, scientists at the Centre for Applied Microbiology and Research at Porton Down supplied the 51,000 British forces with vaccines against anthrax and plague. It took a frenzied effort. "We worked 24 hours a day for several weeks with armed guards patrolling the place," recalls one insider. How much more difficult to protect, suddenly, an entire population!

Medical countermeasures would help few civilians after a BW attack.

Preparations for a BW terrorist attack could, however, be more advanced than they are now. As well as familiarising doctors with BW agents and their symptoms, Colonel Franz advises monitoring levels of diseases so that unusual outbreaks can be noticed quickly, and their severity hopefully reduced by rapid action from the authorities.

Aerosol attack

If an attack were made in the form of an aerosol, it might be possible for some people and animals to avoid exposure to the agent by taking shelter in their homes or offices. This, apparently, is the basis on which civil emergency planning for BW attacks in the UK is carried out. Most BW agents die quickly after they are released (anthrax spores are an exception), so the hope must be that, by the time people are told they may emerge from their shelter, most of the danger will have passed. This does, of course, assume prior knowledge of the attack.

Masks could be useful, although there seems to be no current plan for issuing gas masks to civilians. "As far as I'm aware," says one emergency planning officer, "they don't exist." It may well be, however, that relatively simple oro-nasal masks could help to protect against a BW attack. A paper prepared for the Institute for Defense Analyses in Virginia[7] argues that for populations protected by such masks, the BW threat can be made several orders of magnitude less than that posed by nuclear weapons, whereas for unprotected populations, the BW threat would be greater than the nuclear one.

The rationale for the simple mask is that it would protect against most BW agents, which are breathed in. The masks can be far simpler than those used against chemicals because the filters that remove biological particles are easier to design and make than filters which remove chemicals. The sorts of masks the IDA paper recommends are sold in hardware shops for protecting people who work in dusty environments. The biological defence establishment at Porton Down tested a similar one, which cost only four dollars, during preparations for the Gulf War. Even it allowed leakage of only 0.2 percent of the particles that would be hazardous during a BW attack. The authors of the IDA paper see masks as a way of reducing exposure to BW agents to levels which vaccines have been designed to cope with. They recommend that masks be used in conjunction with shelters, warning systems and vaccines, to blunt the effects of BW attacks. According to a spokesman for the UK Ministry of Defence, the MOD has taken note of the masks as being a useful addition to the advice it could give in helping local authorities or other governments to protect civilians from breathing in biological agents. But whether the masks could be acquired and distributed quickly enough is open to question.

The authors of the IDA paper warn, however, that these masks are not in any case the complete answer to biological protection. They would not give any protection against agents on civilians' clothes or hands, or in their hair. Advances in biotechnology may result in BW agents that could attack through the skin. And BW attacks could still cause huge damage. Even if a city of a million inhabitants were able to save 95 percent of its population through adequate BW defence, it would still suffer 50,000 casualties.

At the moment, the sophisticated defence programmes run by the military would primarily benefit the armed forces. They could provide assistance to the emergency forces too; but—unless the attack were anticipated and the agent known—only very limited protection to civilians.

As far as military personnel go, there are various ways in which countries seek to defend their soldiers against biological warfare. They can develop missiles such as the Patriot system deployed in Saudi Arabia during the Gulf War to shoot down the Iraqi Scuds. They can attack the enemy's launch and storage sites for biological weapons. Other defence measures depend on understanding the nature of agents that may be used against them; for this is a crucial part of developing means of countering them. Logical though this is, it has led many to argue that defensive programmes are bedevilled by a problem: how can countries be sure that others' efforts to understand agents are not a precursor to using them, rather than defending against them? While some are convinced that this dilemma is real, others vehemently deny it. This chapter will look at this debate in more detail later on. First, though, it describes some of the relatively sophisticated measures taken to protect troops.

DEFENSE FOR THE ARMED FORCES

In the UK, defence efforts against biological warfare are concentrated at the Protection and Life Sciences Division (PLSD) of the Ministry of Defence's Defence and Devaluation Research Agency (DERA) at Porton Down, near Salisbury in Wiltshire. The wide range of scientists it employs (chemists, geneticists, biochemists, microbiologists, mathematicians, physicists, doctors, pathologists, immunologists, engineers, computer scientists, operations analysts, geographers and meteorologists) gives some idea of the complexity of defensive measures.

PLSD assesses the hazards posed by possible BW agents: evaluates which ones might be used against UK forces and how dangerous they would be. This involves research into the properties of agents; whether they could be produced on a sufficient scale; whether they would be stable enough for storage and dissemination; and how much would be needed to produce a specific effect. Further research is done into the toxicity of agents; how they would affect the body; whether toxic concentrations could be achieved in a conflict; how the aggressor could deliver the payload; and how different geographical and meteorological conditions would affect delivery. During the Gulf War, the Porton defence establishment realised that it knew a lot about the geography and meteorology of NATO/Warsaw Pact scenarios, but not enough about the Persian Gulf. It has since introduced the Biological, Radiological and Chemical Information System (BRACIS)—a portable computer which predicts the path of a contaminant and the area in which it will form dangerous concentrations. It then overlays on the map a list of the units that are within the danger areas, and estimates how long it will be before the agent reaches the units and how long it is likely to stay.

This was not the only area of the defence establishment's activities that was given extra urgency by the Gulf War. Another of its roles is to detect and identify biological agents in the field. Troops need to be warned of the presence of agents before they are concentrated enough to be harmful. NATO forecasts that if an anthrax warhead were delivered by Scud missile, it would reduce by 90 percent the effectiveness of forces downwind who had no notification of the attack; whereas with notification their effectiveness would be reduced by only 20 percent.[8] The British detectors that were in use before the Gulf War did not provide audible alarms and did not extend to the range of agents that Iraq was suspected of having. They were rapidly improved to deal with conditions in the Gulf. But British forces in the Gulf were in a better position to detect biological agents than the Americans. They had no on-site means at all: a state of affairs which worried their commanders. General Colin Powell, Chairman of the Joint Chiefs of Staff, testified to the US Congress after the Gulf War that "of all the various weapons of mass destruction, biological weapons are of the greatest concern to me."[9]

Whether or not as a result of experiences in the Gulf War, the US government is pouring more money into biological defence. The Pentagon's Defense Advanced Research Projects Agency (DARPA) announced in 1996 that it was recruiting biological warfare defence experts under what might become a £50-million a year initiative to combat "one of the greatest threats" to national security.[10]

Although it is not yet possible to identify agents in aerosols—they have to be collected onto a surface or into a liquid for that—their presence can be detected when they are airborne. Both American and British forces now have the capability for doing this, and each country is building it into an integrated system designed to detect, collect and identify agents in the field. The British system detects particles by examining their behaviour in a beam of light. This determines their shape: the target particles show up as being different from the background. The current instrument can analyse 10,000 particles per second in the 1–10 micron range (the ones most likely to be inhaled and retained in the lungs). The particles are then collected together and another instrument, under development, determines whether biological material is present by detecting chemicals that all living cells contain.[11] Agents are finally identified by determining which antibodies they react with. This three-tier system makes up the Integrated Biological Detection System, which is expected to enter service during 1998. It should be able to identify agents within two or three minutes.

There are other ways of identifying BW agents. The one which holds out most promise is the gene probe, mentioned above. It identifies agents by being configured to react with a unique sequence of their nucleic acid. This identification is extremely specific and can be used on inactivated agents as well as live ones. Toxins do not contain nucleic acid, and therefore the probe needs to be configured for the micro-organism that produces the toxin rather than the toxin itself. Probes can also identify "designer" agents, made by genetic engineering. In association with another scientific advance which amplifies the DNA in a sample so that specific sequences can be more easily detected, gene probes have been developed to the point where they can identify the species and assess the potential virulence of clean samples of the principal pathogens relevant to biological weapons. Portable, automated equipment is expected to achieve this by the turn of the century. Dirty samples and those needing more precise identification (of strains rather than species) are more complicated to develop, but can be done at specialist laboratories.

Until recently, gene probes enabled bacteria to be more quickly identified than viruses could be; but during 1996 another technique called mass spectrometry (which reveals chemical structure) enabled scientists at Porton Down to identify viruses "instantly."[12] The editor of the *International Defense Review*, Clifford Beal, in an up-beat assessment, predicts that "in a decade's time, nothing need take NATO forces by surprise on the potential biological battlefield."[13]

Once an attack has been detected, soldiers must scramble into protective clothing. In the Gulf War this meant suits, respirators, gloves and overboots. Some argue that oro-nasal masks, described above, are attractive for protecting troops without the burden of current protective clothing. However the Ministry of Defence, according to a spokesman, has decided not to procure them for military use because it judged them unable to do anything that the current S10 respirator does not already do better. But more comfortable protective suits may be on the way. Instead of the six layers worn in the Gulf War—not exactly comfortable in desert conditions—a more modern concept is reducing this to two.

The other main category of defensive research is in medical countermeasures. The goal of PLSD research is to provide a vaccine that will be effective against a wide range of biological agents. However vaccination is not without its problems. As well as the complications described above, vaccines, along with many other aspects of defence, are part of the problem of perception.

THE PROBLEM OF PERCEPTION

Vaccines are obviously necessary for troops who may be exposed to BW agents. But exposed in what role?—as defenders or aggressors? If a country is planning to use BW against an enemy, it would vaccinate its own troops before the attack so they would not be affected by any agent that blew back over or otherwise contaminated them. So, while the manufacture of vaccines can be innocent, it can also signal preparations for a BW attack. Similar arguments can be made about other defensive preparations against BW or innocent microbiological research. Botulinum toxin is used to treat muscle spasms such as facial tics by paralysing the abnormal muscles (and recently has been used to paralyse muscles whose spasms cause sweaty palms and vaginismus); ricin has been used to kill cancer cells. As Professor Erhard Geissler, of the Bioethical Research

Group at the Max-Delbruck Centre for Molecular Medicine in Berlin, states: ". . . pathogens and toxins considered for biological and toxin warfare purposes occur in nature, and work for peaceful purposes can be difficult to distinguish from that for hostile purposes. Consequently, much of the work for peaceful and for military purposes can be difficult to distinguish."[14] History provides grisly confirmation. The Japanese were able to hide their biological warfare experiments by labelling the duties of its now-notorious Unit 731 as "study on bacteria, water supply for each unit of Kwantung Army, supply of serum and vaccine, work for preventive medicine, and training of soldiers."[15] This added up to work for prophylactic, protective or other peaceful purposes—allowed by the 1972 Biological Weapons Convention.

The fact that defensive programmes can be mistaken for offensive ones does not mean, of course, that they are actually being subverted for offensive purposes. As of October 1999, 144 countries had made a commitment under the Biological Weapons Convention to dissociate themselves from offensive activities. We have to believe that most of these countries take this obligation seriously. Nevertheless, two of them (Iraq and Russia) are already known to have developed biological weapons in spite of their adherence to the treaty, and the US believes that "twice as many countries now have or are actively pursuing offensive biological weapons capabilities as when the Convention came into force."[16] The Convention allows defensive programmes, and the fact that they are being pursued against this background highlights two very contentious questions: whether they might bring about the very proliferation they seek to prevent, and just how much defence they can provide.

PROLIFERATION?

Some authors argue that the final result of defensive programmes "may well be a biological arms race."[17] The means of production of vaccines demonstrates, they argue, just how close defensive and offensive research are. Vaccines are usually inactivated forms of the virus itself, so a country wanting to develop the vaccine must first grow the virus. Outlining the steps that would be necessary for BW defence, Jonathan King, Professor of Molecular Biology at the Massachusetts Institute of Technology, and molecular biologist consultant Dr Harlee Strauss, write: "These steps—the generation of a potential BW agent, development of a vaccine against it, and testing of the efficacy of the vaccine—are all components that would be associated with an offensive BW program. It is not that the programs "appear" similar; it is that they have many of the same components."[18] King and Strauss argue that the defence/offence problem goes much wider than the production of vaccines. "The blurring of defensive and offensive programs is not limited to research," they write, "but extends to development, testing, production and training. Although it may be possible to use the scale of the project as an indicator of the intent at the development stage and beyond, there is a large grey area where offensive and defensive needs will be indistinguishable."[19] (Where sabotage attacks are concerned, of course, the distinction of scale becomes meaningless. Very small quantities of BW agent can infect very large numbers of people. One gram of anthrax produces enough spores for 100 million lethal doses.)[20]

If defensive and offensive research are hard to distinguish, the argument goes, some people will not believe declarations that research is innocent. Suspicion is easily awoken and difficult to allay. Countries who mistrust others may decide to develop or expand their own BW programmes. Thus defence programmes may encourage the very activities they are designed to prevent. This was in fact what happened between 1915 and 1945, when Germany, France, the USSR and Britain and her allies began developing their own BW programmes.[21]

The intention of the Biological Weapons Convention is, however, clear. Defensive research is permitted; preparations for war are banned. But how, in practice, should the line be drawn?

Another American view is that it can be drawn quite clearly. Dr David Huxsoll is the former commander of the US Army Medical Institute of Infectious Diseases at Fort Detrick, Maryland, which is at the heart of the United States' BW defence. "The only similarities between defensive and offensive research are that common laboratory techniques are used in each at the outset" he writes; "but even at the outset, the experimental hypotheses are diametrically opposed."[22] He continues: "An offensive program would include research programs on mass producing or storing large quantities of micro-organisms, on stabilisation in an aerosol, on improving viru-lence or persistence, or on methods for dissemination and weapon development. In contrast, defensive research comprises develop-ment of biological agent detection methods, treatment and protec-tion, and decontamination capability."

It is clear that professionals in the defence industry and commen-tators on the subject have very different views about the value of defence. Many of their arguments result from their assumptions and perceptions; and in these, safety and openness play a large part.

SAFETY AND OPENNESS

If people doubt whether defensive research is safe, they will be sus-picious of it. As Chapter 5 recounts, between 1949 and 1969, the Pentagon conducted 239 open air biological warfare tests over pop-ulated areas in the US, including San Francisco, Minneapolis, St Louis, Key West and Panama City. The tests were to see how bacte-ria could be spread and how they would behave in a biological at-tack. Instead of pathogenic bacteria, the army used simulants which they insisted were harmless; and—although this is dis-puted—on the basis of knowledge available at the time, they no doubt held this belief in good faith. But evidence, some of it cir-cumstantial, has since been produced that they were not as harm-less as the authorities assumed.

There are also allegations that, even today, micro-organisms the army might use in open-air tests are potentially harmful.[23] Many people—especially those living near the Dugway testing area—are nervous about accepting current assurances on safety. There have been attempts to involve citizens in testing protocols: for example, the setting up in 1989 of the Citizens Advisory Committee for Dug-way Testing. However its members complain that the army has never enabled it to fulfil its role or included it in any meaningful way in discussions.

One way of minimising mistrust of defensive programmes may be to keep them as open as possible. While Dr Huxsoll believes that "the US program is a model of openness in its sharing of informa-tion . . ."[24] others disagree. Charles Piller and Keith Yamamoto, for example, applied to the US Department of Defense for details of biotechnology research projects it funded. On the basis of the incomplete information they were given, they analysed 329 projects funded between 1980 and 1986. One-third of the in-house military projects had potentially offensive applications: for example, creating novel BW agents, investigating aerosol delivery of BW agents, and defeating vaccines. Piller and Yamamoto comment that the result of the military's penchant for secrecy has been "to veil, if not black out, any detailed independent analysis of the BW program—to the peril of US and international security."[25] They also point out that the lack of openness casts doubts on the defensive nature of the policy. There is no explanation about how one element of research is related to another, and this can arouse suspicion. They cite, for example, two projects at different institutions on different aspects of the agent that causes anthrax. Considered separately, these projects sounded quite innocent; but the authors wondered if they could be used together to prevent the diagnosis of an anthrax infection. This could be useful for any country intending to use anthrax aggressively.

When any institution can conduct its activities in secret, dangers can arise. A Congressional Inquiry held at the end of the 1980s found a "disturbing record of safety problems" at military biological (and chemical) research facilities.[26] This in spite of the fact that the army, in its submissions to the inquiry, gave itself a clean—a glowing—bill of health, citing "adequate protection for the workforce and virtually total protection for the external environment."[27] Leonard Cole describes how the army's conclusion was not swayed by extensive doubts expressed by the public. Criticisms of the army's biological research programme, made then and since in other official reports, included: no structure for overseeing safety; no safety inspections; unreported fires and accidents; viruses gone missing (2,352 milliliters of Chikungunya virus from Fort Detrick in 1981 and never recovered); unnecessary duplication of research with civilian agencies; and inadequate safety measures.[28]

It is hardly surprising that there is a lot of scepticism about the safety of the Army's research into biological defence. One way of shaking away its complacency and building up trust would be to be more open about its activities: to treat the Citizens Advisory Committee and its successor, the Technical Review Committee, in the spirit in which they were set up, so that expert civilians could participate in overseeing the testing programme.

There is even more secrecy in Britain than in the United States; but as in the United States, the British authorities claim that there is no unnecessary secrecy in the BW defence programme. The former director of the biological defence establishment at Porton Down, Dr Graham Pearson, maintains: "We are in the business of protecting the British armed forces against the threat of chemical or biological weapons. If we prepared a long and detailed list, this would tell a potential aggressor precisely what it was you were trying to do. It would also tell him what you were not doing."[29] It is obvious that the military is not going to allow total openness about its research programmes. It might try, however, to make sure that as much research as possible can be funded by civilian sources, so that the results can remain in the open literature. During the 1980s, US funding of biological research switched unnecessarily to the military. According to Malcolm Dando, Professor of International Security at the University of Bradford, this resulted in a lot of suspicion. He labels as "sensible" arguments that "military funding should be restricted as far as possible in order that openness is believed in as well as operating . . ."[30]

Much of the research the British Ministry of Defence supports is done in universities, research institutes and industry, and is published in the open literature. As at 9 January, 1996, the Porton defence establishment had 53 extramural contracts, of which 42 were with 21 universities. Their total value was about £5 million, and their duration varied from several months to a few years. None was classified. However, only nineteen contractors, spread across nine universities, were willing to have their relationship to the establishment known.[31] This no doubt has a lot to do with the threats from animal rights extremists—many scientists whose work has nothing to do with defence are unwilling to talk about their research for the same reason—but if greater openness is one way of putting unnecessary suspicions to rest, scientists ought to be willing to justify their contracts, and their methods, publicly. Silence, however wrongly, only fuels suspicion where suspicion already exists.

Occasionally, researchers object to accepting money from the defence budget at all. Molecular biologist Jonathan King of the Massachusetts Institute of Technology is one of about 800 US scientists who have signed a pledge not to do such research. They may be worried that the research will be driven by military rather than civilian interests; that defensive research will have offensive potential; that it will be impossible to know how the research fits into the broader picture and therefore how it might be used; and that doing research in this area may create mistrust and encourage other countries to develop their own BW programmes.

Soldiers in armed conflicts have the right to expect that they will be protected, as far as possible, from the weapons of the other side. This means that defensive programmes against biological warfare are necessary. The perceptions these give rise to ought to be taken seriously, as perceptions influence behavior just as much as facts. Military scientists ought therefore to try to build public confidence in their work. They could do this by admitting when they have made mistakes in the past and being as open as possible about their current research. Scientists in civilian research institutions also ought to be open about and willing to defend the projects they carry out for the defence effort.

At the same time, all countries should make every effort to outlaw biological weapons. The UK, along with many other countries, is trying to strengthen an international regime to stop the proliferation of BW. The next chapter takes a closer look at these efforts, and asks whether they are likely to succeed.

COULD DO BETTER

In 1991, the US Army's Biological Defense Research Programme was accused of wasting nearly half of its annual £30 million budget. A report drawn up by the General Accounting Office and published by the Government Affairs Committee asserted that money was being wasted on misdirected projects and duplication. Charged Senator John Glenn (D-Ohio): "While the BDRP was funding research and development efforts directed against 'exotic' human pathogens in the 1980s, it failed to produce medical countermeasures against many 'conventional' biological agents, such as a vaccine against anthrax."[32]

As well as misdirecting its research, the program was said to have funded research on projects already under way at other federal agencies. Army researchers worked on 19 agents already being studied at the National Institutes of Health and seven diseases targeted by the Centers for Disease Control.

According to the report, cutting down army secrecy and increasing co-ordination of army and civilian research programmes would help to reduce this sort of waste. In fact, the General Accounting Office urged the Army to co-ordinate its research with other federal agencies. Co-operation is needed, it said, not only between medical programmes but between them and the intelligence agencies. "We have to have some sort of relationship between what our intelligence tells us about what efforts should be made to develop biological agents and what our laboratories are doing," said Elisa D. Harris, senior research analyst at the Brookings Institution in Washington. "There has to be a real link between the threat and the defense program."

QUIRKY REALITIES

The 1999 outbreak of West Nile virus in New York, described in the Introduction to this book, illustrated the difficulties in preparing for defense against biological warfare. The initial identification of the virus was mistaken because the scientist at the federal Centers for Disease Control and Prevention (CDC), to whom samples were sent for identification, only checked his samples for antibodies against six viruses commonly found in the United States. Evidently it did not occur to him to check for viruses, such as West Nile, never before seen in the US. Again, in all their plans to detect and handle a sudden outbreak of disease, Federal officials have always assumed that the health professionals primarily involved would be working in human medicine. In fact, Dr Tracey McNamara, who played a major role in the correct identification of the virus, was employed by Bronx Zoo and worked with animals. Plans for responding to outbreaks of disease caused by animals are "not very well resolved," according to Michael Samuel, a research project leader at the National Wildlife Health Center, a unit of the Department of Interior. "I don't know that we as a nation have a contingency plan in place," he said.

Finally, the outbreak underlined the differences in actual human behaviour compared with official plans for a biological defense emergency. Official plans make logical use of the structures in place. What actually happened was that the people involved in the New York outbreak used whatever means they could to find out what was happening, and these were not necessarily those predicted on paper. Dr McNamara sent bird samples for analysis to the CDC in Atlanta; but scientists there were busy identifying the virus that was killing New Yorkers and did not at first link it with the (same) virus responsible for the bird deaths. They therefore gave Dr McNamara's samples lower priority, and did not return her calls for a week. Having recently been to the wedding of a pathologist at the US Army Medical Research Institute for Infectious Diseases, which does not normally become involved in civilian work, she was able to prevail on that lab to look at her samples. Thus the virus, whose appearance the CDC later ascribed to "Mother Nature," was first diagnosed correctly by military rather than by civilian scientists.

A similar twist occurred after the CDC's mistaken diagnosis. At that time, New York state health officials met with scientists from the University of California at a conference, and sent samples to the California lab for analysis without telling the CDC or New York City officials. A month into the outbreak, the California lab came up with the correct diagnosis and the state officials announced they were taking over the situation. The action underlined the tension between city and state officials, whose relations have been described by Dr Stephen C. Joseph, the city's Health Commissioner from 1986 to 1990, as "porcupines making love."

In the event, neither of these anomalies make any difference to the way the city handled the outbreak; but they show that reality is generally more complicated and nuanced than official plans allow for. The initial lack of coordination between New York City health officials could, said health experts, give rise to its own sorts of hazards, with New Yorkers confused about who was responsible for what. "It gives the perception that officials don't know what they're doing; and if people don't have confidence in the people who are responsible for their well-being, that makes for rumours and people saying ridiculous things" said former CDC scientist Charles Calisher.

The whole episode pointed to another lesson, too. "It is a sobering, not so reasuring, demonstration of the inadequacies of the US detection network for emerging disease," said Alan P. Zelicoff, senior scientist at the Center for National Security and Arms Control at Sandia National Laboratories, New Mexico. It also highlighted the relatively small amounts of money currently spent on detecting outbreaks of disease, compared with the hundreds of millions being allocated to biodefense efforts. It may well be that investing more in monitoring all outbreaks of disease is the best way to gain fast warning of biological warfare attacks.

9

INTERNATIONAL REGULATION

The 1990s have seen progress in the international regimes that govern nuclear and chemical weapons. In 1995, the Nuclear Non-Proliferation Treaty was extended indefinitely; in 1996, the Complete Test Ban Treaty was opened for signature; and the Chemical Weapons Convention came into force in April 1997. Biological weapons are the only weapons of mass destruction whose regulation has not been strengthened. Many fear that rogue states may turn to them if regulation is not tightened.

Although governments round the world have long recognized the dangers of biological warfare, their attempts to control them have still only resulted in a very weak regime. This chapter summarizes the arrangements they have put in place, their shortcomings, and how they might be improved. The next chapter asks what concerned people can do to support these efforts to make the world a safer place.

THE 1925 GENEVA PROTOCOL

The Geneva Protocol continued efforts begun in the nineteenth century to try to lessen the horrors of war. It prohibited the use of "bacteriological" (biological) methods of warfare, but enabled states who agreed to abide by its regime to limit this undertaking to other states who also bound themselves by it. Thus it did not represent a universal prohibition, but rather a promise not to be the first to use biological weapons.

THE BIOLOGICAL WEAPONS CONVENTION

The Biological Weapons Convention (BWC) is the current focus of nations' efforts to control the spread of biological weapons. It was opened for signature in 1972 and entered into force in 1975. By October 1999, 144 countries had ratified it, and a further 18 had signed but not ratified. The fact that Egypt and Syria are amongst those 18 is a cause for concern: the Middle East is an unstable region. More worrying still is Israel's status. It has neither signed nor ratified. (Countries agree to abide by an international agreement in two stages. The first is to sign it, which signals their intention to abide by it. The second stage is to ratify it. This means to make the treaty binding under domestic law: in the UK, being passed by Parliament, for example, or in the USA, being approved by two-thirds of the Senate present. Countries which have both signed and ratified an agreement are called States Parties to that agreement: here abbreviated to parties.)

The BWC is an odd agreement: the first which outlaws a whole class of weapons. Yet it has no provisions at all for checking that the parties are keeping to their word. This is worrying, as about eight of them (including China, Iraq, Iran and Libya) are suspected of developing biological weapons, and Russia is known to have them. "Overall, the United States believes that twice as many countries now have or are actively pursuing offensive biological weapons capabilities as when the Convention went into force," said a US representative at the end of 1996.[1] The Convention also teeters precariously between trying to make sure that biology can be used for peaceful purposes, on the one hand, and attempting to eliminate its misuse on the other. Given the dual-use dilemma at the heart of biological weaponry (that is, that the same procedures and equipment are used in the civilian biotechnology industry as to make biological weapons—see Chapter 5), this balancing act is inevitable. It does, however, complicate the BWC's effectiveness, which is further weakened because it has no standing body to administer it. This means that its regime has only been slowly implemented.

Compared with other international treaties, the BWC is a very slight document: a short preamble and just fifteen articles. It is often contrasted with the Chemical Weapons Convention (CWC), which entered into force in April 1997. The CWC is two hundred pages long (to the BWC's four), took nine years to negotiate (to the BWC's three) and contains long and detailed verification provisions to check that parties are behaving according to their obligations. The reasons why the BWC is so much the junior partner are still discussed.

BACKGROUND TO THE BWC

Some commentators suggest that, with the winds of detente blowing through the international arena at the end of the sixties, the superpowers wanted to begin serious discussions on limiting nuclear arms and were happy to get the minor question of BW, which they did not take seriously as militarily useful weapons, out of the way first. The UK had in 1968 suggested a separate treaty on biological weapons—until then they had always been considered along with chemical weapons—and the US renounced its biological weapons capability in 1969. The Soviets, at first opposed to the idea of a separate treaty, fell into line and the deed was done. This benign understanding of events might be thought to explain the lack of verification provisions: after all, if nobody would be bothered to make BW, there would be no point in checking up on them. But this interpretation contrasts with what other commentators are now arguing: that, far from regarding BW as of negligible military importance, the superpowers realised only too well what cheap mass destruction they represented. They had other military options they could use, and they wanted to stop other countries developing a biological capability. The superpowers may have wanted to include verification provisions, but detente did not go that far. As Alexander V. Vorobiev, of the Permanent Mission of the Russian Federation to the Conference on Disarmament has written, ". . . at the time [the BWC] was negotiated the establishment of an effective mechanism to verify compliance was out of the question."[2]

Whatever the truth of its gestation, the BWC is a poor runt of a treaty. Attempts to strengthen it have focused on Review Conferences held every five years since it came into force, and on ad hoc groups set up to address specific tasks. This chapter will look at some of these later on; but first summarizes what the Convention itself contains.

PROVISIONS OF THE BWC

Some of the Convention's fifteen Articles make provision for routine treaty matters—which languages it will be published in, for example, and how it can be amended. But the most important Articles support the BWC on the two legs on which it stands.

Its most crucial Article is its first, according to which signatories undertake "never in any circumstances to develop, produce, stockpile or otherwise acquire or attain microbial or other biological agents or toxins . . . that have no justification for prophylactic, protective or other peaceful purposes . . ." There are two things to notice about this: firstly, that research is not prohibited; and secondly, that the Article amounts to allowing peaceful uses of biological agents and toxins, and prohibiting everything else. Thus the BWC bypasses questions of what agents and which items of equipment are legitimate. It focuses instead on intent: the purpose for which any agent or equipment might be used. Article III requires parties not to supply any other countries with "agents, toxins, weapons, equipment or means of delivery" to further illegal purposes.

So much for the disarmament leg of the Convention. Its other leg concerns development. Under Article X, parties undertake "to facilitate . . . the fullest possible exchange of equipment, materials and scientific and technological information for the use of bacteriological agents and toxins for peaceful purposes." The Article also says that the Convention "shall be implemented in a manner designed to avoid hampering the economic or technological development" of parties.

Given the dual-use problem, these two main provisions of the BWC are largely incompatible. Who can say what "exchange of equipment," for example, is for peaceful purposes and what is for making biological weapons, when the same piece of equipment can be used for both? This difficulty need not be a problem if all parties' interests coincide; but they do not.

The Western and developed countries want to strengthen the disarmament leg of the BWC. They do not want to see biological weapons proliferate. They do not like the thought of "poor men's weapons of mass destruction" destabilising a world security system in which their own defence is strong. They are less interested in helping poorer countries to establish their own biotechnology industries (and they argue, with some justification, that there already exist many bilateral and multilateral aid programmes for exactly this purpose).[3] Poorer countries, on the other hand, want to strengthen the development leg of the Convention. Their attitude is that if they forgo biological weapons, why shouldn't they receive the help set out in the BWC to strengthen their own fledgling biotechnology industries?

It is against this fundamental tension that various measures have been taken to strengthen the Convention. The most regular of these have been the Review Conferences.

REVIEW CONFERENCES

Review Conferences have been held in 1980, 1986, 1991 and 1996. At these meetings the parties have considered each Article of the Convention in turn, and have produced a document commenting on the degree to which each one is being implemented. Each Conference has re-emphasised the basic prohibition of the BWC against biological weapons, and has confirmed that the Convention covers all developments in microbiology, biotechnology and genetic engineering. In this way each has reinforced the international norm prohibiting biological warfare without trying to define exactly what agents and what quantities of them would constitute transgression. Russia has argued that more precision would be helpful for verification. However the UK and other Western parties argue that there is no need for such definition—that, as an official has put it, "Like pornography, you'll know non-compliance when you see it."

After the 1986 Conference, parties agreed to a range of confidence-building measures which were broadened in 1991. These asked them to make information available to each other so that they would understand more about each other's research and lessen suspicion. The declarations that were required included what facilities they had for doing biological research that could pose a high risk; the sort of research defensive programmes were doing; any unusual outbreaks of disease that could raise others' suspicions about their activities; national legislation relating to the BWC; past offensive and defensive programmes; and facilities for preparing human vaccines. They were also asked to increase the international co-operation required under Article X, promoting the use of biological research for permitted purposes.

Responses have been very disappointing. Although a majority of parties have made declarations at some time or other, few have done so consistently and many accounts have been incomplete. Also the level of participation of Third World countries has been extremely low.

The disarmament/development tension has affected the workings of the confidence-building measures. Western countries have tended to stress their security implications, whereas developing countries have seen them more in terms of their promise of economic development. Third World countries feel they have not had the support the West should have given them. At the 1991 Review, they expressed their disapproval by preventing the establishment of a tiny, full-time secretariat which could have kept the parties' attention focused on the issues raised by the Convention between the Reviews, and thus helped to make progress.

Independent voices on both sides of the Atlantic are beginning to call for the developed countries to take Article X more seriously than they have in the past. Julian Perry Robinson, for example, in canvassing the options for the future of the BWC, writes: ". . . we in the North may have to take the development obligations of the treaty a great deal more seriously than we have been doing until now."[4] And a senior US expert on biological weapons commented in January 1997, "We need to be more creative and find a way of meeting the developing countries' worries."

Another measure much complicated by the dual-use dilemma and the disarmament/development conundrum is export controls.

EXPORT CONTROLS

Under Article III of the BWC, parties undertake not to supply other states with agents or equipment that could be used for BW purposes. This has led to the imposition of export controls by many parties, including the UK. The initiative grew out of the work of the fifteen-member Australia Group, set up in 1985 to try to prevent the inadvertent supply of materials needed for making chemical weapons. The group grew (in 1996 it had 29 members), and in 1992 took on work aimed at preventing the spread of biological weapons as well.

The idea of export controls may be a good one, but in practice they deeply flawed. The UK legislation (The Export of Goods (Control) Order 1992) requires licences to permit exports of many human pathogens and toxins, animal pathogens, genetically modified micro-organisms and a variety of equipment capable of use in biological manufacturing. A Royal Society Study Group which examined the UK's controls in 1994, reported that the legislation could only achieve a short delay in proliferation at best, as "a determined aggressor would, if need be, produce BW using unsophisticated equipment not on the lists . . ."[5] It criticized the fact that many of the countries specified as needing special attention to what they were importing were developing countries which had not shown any interest in developing BW. Export controls could therefore hinder their economic development, contrary to the BWC. India also made this point specifically at the Fourth Review Conference in November, 1996. The issue is contentious: the US argues that export controls do not in fact hinder development at all. The Royal Society Study Group recommended a more diplomatic approach to the question of export controls, taking more notice of the development needs of poorer countries as well as the potential threat posed by exports. Malcolm Dando, Professor of International Security at Bradford University, also points to the understaffing and weakness of the authorities which try to make export controls work: "With the best will in the world towards the agencies charged with implementing export controls in the Western world, their track record can hardly be said to inspire great confidence in their ability to stem proliferation." He concludes that "while export controls have to be attempted as part of a general control mechanism at the present time, we should not expect too much from them."[6]

It is clear that export controls by themselves will not stop proliferation. Parties to the BWC believe that the most important way of strengthening the regime is a system of verification: some means of making sure that parties are keeping to their treaty obligations.

VERIFICATION

The fact the BWC has no provisions for verification has bedevilled its credibility from the beginning. The parties' efforts to tackle the issue bore fruit at the 1991 Review Conference, which set up a group of governmental experts—called VEREX—which drew up 21 scientifically feasible measures for verification. These included declarations of biological research activity, inspection visits to facilities where research is carried out, and investigations of alleged use of biological weapons. They were considered by the parties at a conference in September 1994. That meeting mandated another Ad Hoc group to draft proposals for a document which would set out a legally binding verification protocol. The hope was that this would be ready for consideration at the Fourth Review Conference in 1996, but it was not.

The Ad Hoc group was also asked to draw up confidence-building measures and ways of strengthening Article X. Progress on these has not had as much attention from the parties as the verification issue, although at least one measure (ProCEID, which we look at later on) has been suggested.

There are many reasons why progress has been slow. Verification is contentious for both political and technical reasons. Even Western nations disagree on certain aspects of it: in fact they have interpreted the term in different ways. The Americans have tended to the view that it is only worth while trying to set up a verification regime if it will produce well-nigh incontrovertible evidence of non-compliance. Given the dual-use problem, and the small scale on which weapons work can be undertaken (and therefore the ease of doing it secretly), the Americans have until recently argued that no effective verification is possible—and are still reluctant even to use the word. Although the Commerce and Defense departments are still sceptical, President Clinton announced in 1996 that he would support efforts to negotiate the protocol. It was not, however, until 1998 that he used his State of the Union Address to articulate his support for "a new international inspection system to detect and deter cheating." At about the same time, the US drew up a more detailed idea of what it would regard as an acceptable protocol, and prepared to take a more active part in the negotiations.

In July of that year, the US government put its name to a document drawn up by 29 governments on the final day of the eleventh session of the Ad Hoc Group meeting, agreeing on the need to "pursue the early and successful conclusion of the Ad Hoc Group negotiations as a matter of urgency." The US idea of what would constitute an acceptable regime, however, has differed markedly from that of states in the European Union.

The UK has long been keen to have verification. It takes a more nuanced view of what is meant by it, accepting that it is only one component within a treaty regime that can build confidence in compliance. It may, according to the UK, be enough to be able to judge work in progress plausible, with no signs of anything unusual that might indicate illegal activity. What is needed, according to a government official, is to be able to go round a facility and see what is going on there. If it all hangs together, and there is no intelligence which raises suspicions, inspectors could be confident enough that the facility was within the BWC regime to make it a worth while exercise. And the knowledge that facilities would be inspected might be enough to put a potential aggressor off. France and Germany share this view.

One of the main difficulties is the attitude of the pharmaceutical industry. It worries about the costs of verification and about commercial secrecy. Some see verification as an excuse for some people to spy on others' biotechnology secrets. This is the attitude of the US biotechnology and pharmaceutical industries, as well as Third World countries, which foresee teams of Western inspectors invading their establishments while they would not be on the teams inspecting Western facilities. The conditions under which inspectors could come into any facility, and whether there might have to be a *prima facie* case for the need for inspection to be established first, are further points of discussion.

The American industry's position is sadly different from, and often compared to, that with the Chemical Weapons Convention (CWC). The US chemical industry was intimately involved in contributing to the negotiation of a verification regime for the CWC, and relations between the industry and government have prospered. It has not been so with BWC verification and the pharmaceutical industry. Unfortunately, Russian delegations were given more access to US commercial facilities than the industry wanted in an inspection exercise in the early 1990s. That seems to have soured relations between the industry and government, and there has been no appreciable change since. However, the US position on the negotiations takes the pharmaceutical industry's suspicions on board and has been completely opposed to all visits except ones initiated by the receiving state. It remains to be seen whether the US will accept some compromise on this issue, as other Western states see some form of mandatory visits as crucial for deterring clandestine and illegal developments.

A verification protocol is at last taking shape, even though it still has many points remaining to be agreed. It provides for mandatory declarations of the most relevant facilities (military and military-related bio-defence programmes and facilities; high containment facilities; work with listed pathogens and toxins; aerobiology/aerosol dissemination; production microbiology). This would be followed by infrequent visits to ensure that declarations were complete and accurate; and investigations if there were a concern that a state was non-compliant. At the end of 1999 there was significant progress on this front, with wide acceptance of a package of non-confrontational visits that could be made to ensure that a country's declarations were accurate and complete. Such visits would be completely separate from investigations that would be carried out if any country's activities fell under suspicion.

Another difficult area which is also now seeing some progress is international cooperation in biotechnology for peaceful purposes, specifically for the benefit of developing countries. Many of these have been reluctant to bear the cost of a verification regime when they do not see biological weapons as an immediate threat to their security. The protocol includes proposals for assistance with biosafety, information on research programmes using biological agents for peaceful purposes, and surveillance and reporting of infectious diseases around the world.

It is hoped that a verification protocol will be finalised and adopted by a special conference of States Parties in 2000, in time for the Fifth Review Conference in 2001. The achievement would be a fitting 75th anniversary of the 1925 Geneva Protocol, the first international attempt specifically to prohibit the use of "bacteriological methods of warfare."

INDUSTRIAL CONCERNS

The pharmaceutical industry in both the US and the UK has felt threatened by verification proposals and on-site inspections. As mentioned above, its prime worry is about confidentiality. How can it be sure that an inspection team might not obtain and misuse commercial secrets? According to Dr Rob Imrie of SmithKline Beecham Pharmaceuticals, the industry is worried on various counts.[7] Public disclosure of critical information could render patent applications invalid; information about manufacturing processes, the scale of operations or market-sensitive information could be of value to competitors; and the inspection would cause disruption and perhaps even loss of production batches. Another worry is that the media could get the wrong end of the stick and, assuming that there would be no inspection smoke without non-compliance fire, produce bad publicity for the company.

Another crucial concern is the sampling of whatever is being produced, to verify its identity. Dr Imrie writes: ". . . a living cell may well be the result of many years of research effort . . . Unlike a sample of a chemical, a small number of viable cells can be sufficient to build up stocks necessary for commercial production . . ." Moreover, "modern genetic analytical techniques are now capable of abstracting information of value from dead cells."[8] For these reasons, he argues that no samples should be taken off-site.

These and other worries have been addressed by a series of mock inspections carried out at four UK facilities (one of which was a research and development pilot plant managed by Dr Imrie) between 1993 and 1994. The inspections were initiated by government officials, and the companies who own the plants volunteered to have them inspected. None has any military connection. Apart from the pilot plant, they were a large-scale pharmaceutical production plant, a pharmaceutical research and development/production plant and a vaccine plant.

The "inspectors" did their job over two days, hosted at each plant by a home team consisting of government advisors and company personnel. There were problems, foreseen and unforeseen; but the official conclusion at the end of the exercise was that in-depth inspections are practicable and the risks to commercially sensitive information can be reduced to an acceptably low level.[9] This was also the conclusion of two later random visits, carried out by Austria and the Nordic group of countries, to industrial facilities. Similarly, experts at the University of Bradford Biological Weapons Convention Project have concluded that "the numbers of facilities that will need to be declared will be of the order of 10s per country, the information to be declared will not require any disclosure of commercial proprietary information and the level of detail and amount of information required in the envisaged declarations will not be an undue burden on what is already a highly regulated industry.[10]

The industry may not be so sanguine; but at least the co-operation between industry and government has led to an understanding of each other's positions and a willingness to work for solutions.

The mock inspections are one of a series of measures and proposals whose purpose is ultimately to strengthen the BWC. Two other proposals should be mentioned as well.

CRIMINALIZING BW

One recent suggestion is that parties should be required to enact domestic legislation criminalizing BW. Article IV of the BWC already requires parties to "take any necessary measures to prohibit and prevent" violations of the treaty anywhere under their jurisdiction, but the obligation not to meddle with biological weapons is still on states rather than on non-state groups such as individuals, companies or ideologically-motivated groups. Chemical and biological weapons expert Julian Perry Robinson, whose idea this is, points out that criminalizing BW under domestic law "can provide a direct and unambiguous threat of criminal prosecution and punishment to deter terrorist . . . groups . . . Moreover, it can increase the vigilance and authority of governments in combating such activities . . ."[11] The US, the UK and Russia have passed laws under which it is a criminal offence to produce or traffic in biological weapons (see Chapter 3); but many others have not.

The Chemical Weapons Convention does have such a criminalizing provision. Perry Robinson maintains that if the Japanese had enacted a domestic law before the Aum Shinrikyo nerve gas attack in 1995, the authorities would have been better able to stop it.

MONITORING DISEASE

Since 1994, the Federation of American Scientists has published a web site which monitors outbreaks of disease world-wide. The rationale is that the better the international civil system of disease monitoring, the less likely it is that deliberately-caused outbreaks will go undetected. Efforts to improve disease monitoring could thus go hand-in-hand with strengthening the BWC. Another proposal on these lines is Pro-CEID (Programme for Countering Emerging Infectious Diseases).[12] This calls for international teams at medical research institutions to be equipped with all the equipment and know-how necessary to produce vaccines against biological agents relevant to the BWC. The hope is that the programme would narrow the technology gap between rich and poor countries and strengthen Article X of the BWC.

None of the proposals so far outlined will by themselves make sure that the biological weapons threat will be contained. But an idea has grown up that a number of measures, taken collectively, might mesh together to deter states from developing their own.

WEB OF DETERRENCE

The idea of a web of deterrence is to make any country thinking of acquiring biological weapons think again. It has been likened to a series of fences difficult to jump, whose cumulative effect would put an aggressor off.[13] The political penalties would be so painful and the military benefits so few that the potential aggressor would see little point in developing a national BW capability. The four elements of the web, which have been elaborated by Dr Graham Pearson (former Director of the biological defence establishment at Porton Down), are effective defence against BW attack, arms control and verification, export controls and, finally, decisive action by the international community when any country breaches its international obligations.

Effective defence for soldiers is improving but it is hard to see how it can include civilians. However, it also includes military means such as ballistic missiles which can intercept incoming warheads. Arms control, the subject of this chapter, has its problems too. Export controls can do little. The international community could do a great deal more. It could work out some legal regime that would mandate countries to take action against others who use weapons of mass destruction. And in the absence of a formal regime, it could make it quite clear that using such weapons is unacceptable. If, for example, there had been an outcry when Iraq used chemical weapons for four years during the Iran-Iraq War, with boycotts of Iraqi exports, might Saddam Hussein have thought twice about developing his biological arsenal? The world community needs to make a stand to reinforce the international norm against using biological weapons.

It is not only the international community in the guise of governments which could do more. Scientists could raise their own and the public's consciousness of the dangers of biological weapons, to add another pressure on governments to sort out and conform to a stricter international regime. We will return to the responsibility of scientists later on.

THE 1996 REVIEW CONFERENCE

The Review Conference took place in the shadow of three important developments since the 1991 Conference. In 1992, the Russians admitted that they had maintained an offensive biological weapons programme. Iraq's offensive programme was gradually uncovered by the dogged determination of the United Nations Special Commission. And March 1995 saw the Japanese sect Aum Shinrikyo carry out a terrorist attack on the Tokyo subway. Although they used gas, it became clear that their weapon of choice had been biological, and that they had been developing biological weapons and testing them in the streets of Tokyo.

These developments might have increased the pressure on the Conference participants to make progress in strengthening the

Convention. However the ad hoc group was not ready to present its verification proposals, and this took the edge off the urgency of the proceedings.

The Conference was very much a holding affair. It could not endorse the key elements of the verification plan, as these were not yet agreed on; nor did it set a deadline by which the verification plan should be ready to be presented to the parties. The Final Declaration did not mention the Aum Shinrikyo by name, although it did urge parties to pass domestic legislation "in order, *inter alia*, to exclude use of biological and toxin weapons in terrorist or criminal activity." Neither did it mention Russia or Iraq by name as having broken their treaty obligations. The usual tensions between the developed and developing countries were apparent, and manifested themselves in a variety of ways. None of these, however, nor the reactions to them, was enough to threaten the work of the ad hoc group which is by far and away the most important activity the parties are engaged on. According to a senior American source, the Review Conference "met the minimalist goal of Do No Harm."

But there were some positive outcomes. The Conference brought supporters of verification some comfort. It was generally very supportive of the verification discussions, and the Final Declaration encouraged the group engaged in them to move on to a negotiating format and fulfil its mandate as soon as possible before the beginning of the Fifth Review Conference, presumably in 2001.

The Conference also reiterated its commitment to Article I; and it specifically added "molecular biology" and "any applications resulting from genome studies" to the list of scientific and technological developments which must not be misused. This wording reinforced the prohibitions added at the Third Review Conference, on the misuse of developments arising from "microbiology, genetic engineering and biotechnology," and was felt to signal the continuing importance the parties attached to the basic purpose of the Convention.

There was one innovation at the Review Conference. For the first time, non-governmental organisations (NGO's) were allowed to make statements, albeit in an informal session. Representatives of the Federation of American Scientists, the Pugwash Conferences on Science and World Affairs, the International Network of Engineers and Scientists for Global Responsibility, and several more, participated. The NGO's do important work, publishing information, airing ideas and making proposals relevant to the governments' efforts. They provide a bridge between governments and citizens who want to inform themselves about biological weapons. The last chapter looks more closely at some of their contributions, and discusses how more people might become involved in pressing for progress to rid the world of biological weapons.

10

BY OPPOSING END THEM

In 1966 a graduate student went to have a chat with Marc Lappe, Professor of Health Policy and Ethics at the Illinois College of Medicine. The young man's field was marine biology. He was an authority on the properties of saxitoxin: one of the most toxic substances known. Made by algae, it can kill people who eat contaminated shellfish. In its purified form, applied to a flechette or other high-velocity missile, it can kill a man in fifteen minutes.

The young scientist had been offered a post-doctoral scholarship at Fort Detrick in Maryland, which at that time carried out both defensive and offensive biological warfare research. He wanted to chew the offer over with Professor Lappe. He was aware that the Detrick laboratories would offer him the best facilities he could find for his research, which was to study the health consequences of ingesting saxitoxin. But there was the nagging possibility that some of his work could conceivably be applied to the offensive programme. Should he accept the scholarship?

He decided to go to Detrick, where he successfully isolated the toxin. Later on, the CIA was alleged to have used it in assassinations.

Professor Lappe argues[1] that the young man should not have gone to Detrick. Although his own work was to tackle a public health problem, he knew that his paymaster was researching into ways of conducting warfare, and therefore that his results could be used for offence. To imagine that he was not responsible for the ends to which others put his work, says Lappe, is "based on the premise that scientific knowledge is morally neutral, and that the eventual uses to which it may be put are outside the ken of even the most percipient researcher. Such a position belies a duty . . . to assess the likelihood that certain knowledge or data will be misused."[2]

Now that the US and the UK have both given up offensive research, questions about scientists' responsibilities are no longer embodied in similar dilemmas. Many argue however that they are uniquely responsible for opposing the misuse of their knowledge.

One such is Sir Joseph Rotblat, winner of the 1995 Nobel Peace Prize. Born in Poland in 1908, and denied an early education because of World War I, he developed an interest in physics through reading science fiction. He enrolled in evening classes available for people without the usual academic qualifications, and by the time he was 30 had made a name for himself in the physics community. Invited to Liverpool University in 1938, he quickly realised the implications of fission experiments he was reading about: the production of electrical energy, and the possibility of the atomic bomb.

Because some of the early fission experiments had been done in Germany, Rotblat feared that the Germans might be working on an atomic bomb of their own. He therefore swallowed his belief that scientists should only work for humanitarian purposes, and went to work on the Manhattan Project which developed the American atomic bomb at Los Alamos. He reasoned that the only way to stop Hitler using such a bomb would be to threaten to retaliate in kind. When, at the end of 1944, he discovered that the Germans were not working on a bomb of their own, he left the Project—the only scientist to do so. After the War, he was instrumental in setting up the Pugwash Conferences on Science and World Affairs, which provided a low-key but high-level forum for scientists from East and West to meet and discuss the consequences of the nuclear arms race, and nuclear arms control and disarmament. These meetings were especially valuable during the suspicious years of the Cold War, when there was hardly any communication between countries on different sides of the Iron Curtain.

Today, Sir Joseph is unequivocal. "Everybody should take responsibility for events, but scientists particularly because of the impact that science and technology have on the whole of society. Nuclear weapons are the prime example—they have changed our whole civilisation. But further development in genetic engineering is also a threat to the whole of humanity. Scientists can foresee bet-

ter than other members of the community the results of their research."[3]

The basis for scientists' particular responsibilities has also been
eloquently argued by Robert L. Sinsheimer, Professor of Biology at
the University of California, Santa Barbara.[4] According to Sinsheimer, scientists are part of three communities: "their national society, the international fellowship of scientists, and the human race,
past, present and future." Historically, he argues, membership of
the national society has dominated the other two loyalties when
scientists have been called to serve its needs. Nationalism has been
stronger than internationalism: "without strong international organisation and large internationally based resources, the obligations of such an allegiance are tenuous . . ."

Sinsheimer points to the third community—the human race—as
the one which may well entail the most acute moral imperative:
"Scientists are aware of the enormous effort humanity has ex-
pended to wrest from nature our present treasure of human knowledge. They understand how this treasure has enabled us to triumph
over animal foes, climatic vagaries, and deadly diseases . . . to expand our intellectual horizons again and again as we gain a truer
vision of our origins and our place in the cosmos, in an unending
task . . ." It is this unique perspective of scientists which gives them
responsibility for nurturing the edifice of knowledge they and their
predecessors have created. Biological weapons, says Sinsheimer,
"represent a perversion of the greatest accomplishments of cumulative generations of scientific endeavour and insight. Their use—
and their development certainly makes possible their use—would
make meaningless the lives of every scientist of every time."

Physicists have had to face this problem. So have chemists: their
subject has also been perverted for war. Biologists need to stop the
militarization of their achievements. What can they do?

CONTRIBUTIONS BY SCIENTISTS

Few working scientists are interested in the issue. Some of those
that are were represented by the non-governmental organizations
(NGO's) which addressed the Fourth Review Conference of the Biological Weapons Convention (BWC) in Geneva in November,

1996. Their statements show their alarm and the practical measures they are taking to make a contribution.

Dr Barbara Hatch Rosenberg, speaking on behalf of the Federation of American Scientists Working (FAS) Group on Biological Weapons Verification, said: "The rate at which bioscience is now developing new technologies with ominous potential for hostile use is truly astounding. These new technologies are surely not being overlooked by military establishments. Should we simply *trust* that they will always be handled benignly?" The FAS has for seven years been studying how verification could be carried out without significantly interfering with any legitimate, peaceful activity. They are convinced it can be done, and their proposals add to the ideas being developed by governments.

The Society of Friends (Quakers) also made a contribution. Its United Nations Office printed and distributed a Briefing Book[5] as a service to all delegations in Geneva. By no means all countries have the resources or expertise to prepare sophisticated inputs into international negotiations, and the Briefing Book was seen as a way of making information about the BWC available to all. David Atwood, on behalf of the Friends World Committee, explained that the Quakers see the BWC as important "in promoting better relations among states and international co-operation in the peaceful uses of microbiology, especially for the prevention of disease. It forms an integral part of our vision of a well-ordered world, a world at peace."

The World Medical Association was another NGO to address the Conference. Dr James Appleyard, of the British Medical Association, voiced doctors' concerns about the threat of genetic weapons. "We reject any arguments that talk of genetic weapons is scaremongering," he said. "We believe that, having regard to the speed at which knowledge is increasing and bearing in mind the trends in legitimate therapeutic research, the necessary scientific knowledge to make genetic weapons feasible is becoming ever closer and may be here by the time of the next Review Conference or the one after that"—i.e., in 2006. Dr Appleyard called for a professional system of scrutiny to guard against misuse of genetic research. "We believe that the scientists involved in any area of scientific research are the most effective guardians of the legitimacy of research developments in that area," he said.

The International Network of Engineers and Scientists for Global Responsibility (INES) also addressed the Conference. On their behalf, Professor Kathryn Nixdorff asked the Conference to "appeal to the scientific community and their associations to support only those activities that have justification for prophylactic, protective or other peaceful purposes, and to refrain from activities that are not in compliance with the BWC."

If such an appeal is made, how do scientists respond?

REACTIONS FROM SCIENTISTS

I wrote to ten UK biological societies,[6] asking them whether they had considered the developments in research that are relevant to biological warfare, and what their role might be in making sure that their particular branch of biology would not be used for aggressive purposes.

Eight replied. None had considered BW in any depth: in fact the only two bodies which had ever mentioned it had done so at the urging of specific members who were professionally involved in the subject. Comments varied from "I've never seen anything about it" to "It's not appropriate for us as a learned society to have views on professional issues." Another society asserted that having a view on the issue would compromise its charitable status; and that if it were to take any stance on biological warfare it would be sure to alienate those members which did not agree with its position. Some organisations said they only looked into questions they were specifically asked about, and they had never been asked about biological weapons: "It's not something we've had to address." Their daily agendas were crowded with everything from nitrates in water to the social and ethical issues of modern medical genetics. They saw biological war as a peripheral matter, especially when so much time now has to be spent raising money for research.

The general feeling about biological war was that it is unlikely. One microbiologist referred to the dangers fading into the background with the ending of the Cold War. Another said he felt that biological weapons couldn't be equated with nuclear or chemical weapons, because of the inherent uncertainty of biological processes. "They [biological weapons] wouldn't be likely to wipe out the whole human race" he said, adding that their dangers were magnified by the media. There was some cheerful agnosticism: "Maybe we're living in a fool's paradise—maybe we're just naive." The societies were keen on the advantages genetic engineering will bring, but very sceptical that it would result in any new "super bug" that would be more deadly than what occurs naturally. They could not however rule that out; and some stressed the enormous strides in modern biotechnology: "Things which we marvelled at three or four years ago, PhD students are doing now."

None felt any responsibility as scientists to be warning of dangers or educating the public. One felt that issues like biological war were too important to be left either to politicians or to scientists, and wished for an intelligent public debate. He would be happy to participate in discussions about biological weapons "if I could actually talk to people without having to write a book about it to get them to understand what I'm saying." The same representative said his organisation's members were not sympathetic to the idea of scientists being involved in public discussions, even though he recognized that scientists were the only people with enough knowledge and understanding to inform the public: "There's quite a lot of neutrality and not a lot of action." Another organization summed up much of the feeling here by saying, "We tend to think of ourselves as scientists first, and talk about the rest over a pint."

Of all the scientific bodies in the UK, the most prestigious is the only one to have addressed any BW issues. In July, 1994, the Royal Society produced a report "to examine how science could contribute to the control of biological weapons."[7] Evidently the Society did not feel hamstrung by the fact that the report might not have reflected the views of all its Fellows, or that it might somehow be compromising their scientific integrity by discussing the subject. Evidently, too, its perception of scientists includes the notion that they are aware of and willing to discuss the uses to which their work is put.

This idea of the role of scientists was spelled out by the then President of the Royal Society, Sir Michael Atiyah, in an Anniversary Address on 30 November, 1995. Speaking in his personal capacity 50 years after the dropping of the atomic bombs on Japan, he reflected on the involvement of scientists in military work and how it elicited a hostile reaction from the general public. "The only way to break down this suspicion and distrust is for scientists to speak out openly and freely, to criticise the establishment when necessary and to demonstrate that independence of thought really is the hallmark of a scientist," he said. He was glad that the Royal Society had produced its report on biological weapons, which, along with other lethal weapons, should be of concern to scientists: "I believe that scientists should speak out on matters such as these. It would be immoral not to."

Even if the ordinary run of scientific societies do not see their role as becoming involved in any sort of debate about the wider uses of their subjects, there should be nothing stopping individual members informing themselves about the issues. None of my respondents pretended to know a great deal about the subject, and some of their opinions underlined the prudence of their modesty (eg, "Personally, I believe [biological weapons] less dangerous in warfare than chemicals . . .").

If the scientific community were to inform itself about the dangers of biological weapons, what might result? Scientific conferences might see fit to have occasional sessions on the subject. This would bring the weight of respected scientists to bear on the issue. They might help stop a feared slide into acceptance of the inevitability of biological warfare.

During the 1980s, various United Nations teams confirmed that Iraq was using chemical weapons against Iran. The Security Council only criticized Iraq once by name, in 1986. The final year of the war brought another UN confirmation (to add to its previous five) that Iraq was using chemical weapons, but the Security Council ignored it. According to the British Ambassador, Sir Crispin Tickell, the Council "didn't want to upset the applecart" by criticising Iraq before peace talks.[8] After the war ended, columnist Flora Lewis observed that the "deafening silence of governments on Iraq's use of chemical weapons" encouraged other countries to develop their own: "The complicity of the world community with Iraq shows that it can be done with impunity."[9] Given the use of chemicals in the Iran-Iraq war, William Webster, director of Central Intelligence, was concerned "that the moral barrier to biological warfare has been breached" as well.[10]

If scientists were to discuss the issue, the press would report it. A more informed public would want to reinforce the revulsion ordinary people feel about the use of biological weapons, and urge governments to protest about the use of any weapons of mass destruction. A public more alive to the threats posed by biological weapons would back up governments trying to strengthen the Biological Weapons Convention. It would signal its support for a stronger regime, and use consumer pressure to encourage the pharmaceutical industry to agree on inspection arrangements to help verification. It would also encourage governments to be imaginative about coping with the fears and needs of the third world: an approach which would, again, help suspicions to lessen and cooperation to grow amongst parties to the Convention. It would keep in mind that scientific developments have repeatedly been put to military use, and agitate for international scrutiny of genetic engineering so that its military potential could be strangled without limiting its legitimate and beneficial uses. It would work towards building up confidence to the point where national defensive programmes might, some time in the future, no longer be seen as necessary. And in all these measures it would affirm its belief that it can act to bring about a safer world.

OPTING OUT

In 1988, cell biologist Dr Sue Mayer was lecturing in the School of Vetinary Science at Bristol University. One of her colleagues was about to accept funding from the Ministry of Defence to carry out some research. As Sue Mayer explained,[11] she and several of her other colleagues objected:

"I was working in a group known as the Aerobiology Group. Our research was on horses, but the horse is a very good model for humans as well. Colleagues were looking at what happens when you breathe in organisms and how they cause disease, and how you could recognize what would be an infectious dose of disease. And that was the work that the MoD were interested in.

"What happens is that when organisms are in air they're quite delicate, and some of them get sub-lethal damage. But then when they're breathed into the respiratory tract, some of them get repaired, and can be active again and so cause disease. And so what the MoD wanted was some research which would represent how lungs work and how they did that repair process, so they'd get an idea of how many organisms are really needed to cause disease. Their stated intention was to be able to use that artificial lung as a kind of a sampler to see if there was an infectious dose of something in the air as a defensive thing. So if they were in the Gulf and not sure whether Saddam was going to use BW against them, they could take an air sample and put it through this portable artificial lung and see whether the bacteria in the air would cause disease. They said openly that this was for defensive purposes for troops in the front line.

"Obviously understanding how the lungs repair sub-lethal damage would help in civilian work as well—in air hygiene, for example—where you might think there was no bacteria in the air that could cause disease, but in fact there really might be. This could be relevant in an infectious ward in a hospital, say, or in a calf house.

"I just didn't feel we should have been doing that sort of research. As it was being funded by the MoD, it wouldn't be restricted to the civilian applications and the future direction of the research would be driven by military interests. I had other worries too—first of all that even in the military sense, it didn't just have defensive potential. In fact someone at the Vet School said at the time, "Well of course it could help you decide just how many bugs to put in a bomb, or how many bugs you need to infect a population." And of course the MoD are only allowed to do defensive research, but we were unable to find out what other research they were doing—so we couldn't get a picture of what they were intending to do. That was one of the things we tried to find out, but that was confidential. And I felt that just doing the research creates mistrust. People think, "If they're doing it, we're going to do it." I had a visit from the Scientific Attache at the Czech Embassy. She offered me trips to Czechoslovakia. I think she thought I'd be a good source of information. I told my MP who told me to dislocate myself rapidly, so I did. You don't expect these things to happen to you—it was like a spy movie.

"I came back from holiday to find there'd been a mass staff meeting of people on the site concerned about it. There was a group of between six and a dozen of us who tried to negotiate out of it. The major reason we were given for the authorities' opposition to us was that if it wasn't research that we were actually going to be doing ourselves, even if was in the group that we worked in, we couldn't interfere with our colleagues' academic freedom to do that research. I found the atmosphere extremely unpleasant—some of the personal unpleasantness and threats I had from people in authority. Basically they threatened legal action for talking to the press. I think in retrospect they couldn't possibly have done that, but when you haven't ever been in that situation before you don't know that they couldn't drag you through the courts, and you're on your own, and you feel very vulnerable even if you aren't really. And the whole way that the university hierarchy closed ranks, didn't want to talk about it, just said it's academic freedom, wouldn't address some of the underlying issues.. I decided I was going to leave. I was quite fortunate that I could get another job because I was a vet quite straightforwardly—it was much easier for me than for others.

"It did dramatically change my perspective on academic life and the interaction between science and politics and policy. It was quite a life-changing experience. I'd thought that I would stay in universities, lecture in therapeutics, research and that would be that. But I became Scientific Director of Greenpeace!—and I'm now an independent science policy consultant. I think I was very naive before: I hadn't really thought about how science is influenced by political agendas and how science participates in that, both knowingly and unknowingly sometimes. And I hadn't realised how strong some of those institutions, like the MoD and the university, are. Although they're meant to be for open speech and discussion, in fact that's only within certain boundaries. And if you step over those boundaries you're not really welcome.

"The research sort of went ahead. It was a big failure, I'm delighted to say! There's never been any more interest in MoD funding work there since. The MoD also seemed to think they didn't want another fuss—so we felt it was very successful in the longer term.

"I went to one of the briefings at the Foreign Office during the Gulf War, after they'd gone into Iraq. They were obviously profoundly shocked when they discovered what the Iraqis' capabilities were. They sent memos round universities saying they should be careful about the projects foreign students worked on. But it's an area you just can't police, and with genetic engineering it adds heaps because you can make what were pretty useless weapons before into something potentially very useful. And that's a bit frightening really."

NOTES

Chapter 1: The Growing Threat

1 V J Derbes. "De Mussis and the Great Plague of 1348. A forgotten episode of bacteriological warfare", *Journal of the American Medical Association,* 196, 1966, pp 59–62.

2 Quoted in *The Problem of Chemical and Biological Warfare,* Volume 1, SIPRI, Almqvist and Wiksell, Stockholm, 1971, p215. For an extended description of the history of BW, see Jean Pascal Zanders, "Dynamics of Chemical Armament", PhD thesis, Faculty of Economic, Social and Political Science, Free University, Brussels, February 1996.

3 *The Laws of Manu,* Ch.7 v.90, translated by Wendy Doniger with Brian K Smith (Penguin Classics).

4 Reported in *A survey of Chemical and Biological Warfare* by John Cookson and Judith Nottingham, Sheed and Ward, 1969, p282.

5 Matthew Meselson, statement before the US Senate Committee on Government Affairs and its Permanent Subcommittee on Investigations, hearings on *Global Spread of Chemical and Biological Weapons,* 17 May, 1989.

6 This name has been attached to this establishment since 1995. From 1991–5 it was known as the Chemical and Biological Defence Establishment (CBDE). Before that it had various names at different times. To avoid confusion, it will be referred to by its geographical location: Porton Down.

7 G B Carter, *Porton Down: 75 Years of Chemical and Biological Research,* HMSO, London, 1992, p74.

8 G. Carter, "Biological warfare and biological defence in the United Kingdom 1940–79", *Royal United Services Institute Journal,* December 1992, pp67–74.

9 The data for this estimate come from J. Reed, *Defence Exports: Current Concerns,* (Jane's Consultancy Services, London, 1993). It was simplified to the form quoted above by Malcolm Dando, *Biological Warfare in the 21st Century,* Brassey's, 1995, pp180–181.

10 *Proliferation of Weapons of Mass Destruction: Assessing the Risks,* Office of Technology Assessment, Washington DC, 1993, OTA-ISC-559.

11 US Congress, Office of Technology Assessment, *Proliferation of Weapons of Mass Destruction: Assessing the Risks,* OTA-ISC-559 Washington DC, August 1993, p11.

12 Douglass, Joseph D., Jr., and Neil C. Livingstone, *America the Vulnerable: the Threat of Chemical and Biological Warfare*, Lexington Books, Lexington MA. 1987.

13 *Chemical and Bacteriological (Biological) Weapons and the Effects of their Possible Use*, United Nations, New York, 1969, p50.

14 David L. Huxsoll et al, "Medicine in Defense Against Biological Warfare", *Journal of the American Medical Association*, Vol 262, No 5, 4 August, 1989.

15 Johannes Nohl, *The Black Death: A chronicle of the plague compiled from contemporary sources*; Unwin, London, 1926, p7.

16 *Ibid*, p18.

Chapter 2: Agents of Biological Warfare

1 Paul Majendie, "Britain Battles Chemical, Biological Horrors of War." Reuters, 31 July 1994.

2 US Congress, Office of Technology Assessment, *Proliferation of Weapons of Mass Destruction: Assessing the Risks*, Washington, DC, August 1993, p53.

3 Jonathan B. Tucker, "The Future of Biological Warfare", in *The Proliferation of Advanced Weaponry*, edited by W. Thomas Wander and Eric H. Arnett, American Association for the Advancement of Science, 1992, p57.

4 These criteria are listed by Malcolm Dando in *Biological Warfare in the 21st Century*, Brasseys, 1996, which is also a source of the different diseases. Another source for these is *FOA informerar om: A Briefing on Biological Weapons*, published by the Swedish National Defence Research Establishment, Umea, 1995. The most comprehensive source remains *CB Weapons Today*, Volume II of *The Problem of Chemical and Biological Warfare*, SIPRI, 1973.

5 These lists and some of the descriptions are taken from *Biological Warfare in the 21st Century* by Malcolm Dando, Brassey's, 1994.

6 The following discussion is based on *FOA informerar om: A briefing on biological weapons*, FOA (Swedish National Defence Research Establishment), Umea, 1995, pp34–40.

7 Graham Pearson, "Chemical and Biological Defence: An Essential National Security Requirement", *RUSI Journal*, August 1995, Vol 140, No 4, pp 20–27.

8 Neil C Livingstone, *The War Against Terrorism*, Lexington Books, Lexington MA, 1982.

9 Professor Harry Smith, personal communication, 7 November 1996.

10 FOA document, *op. cit.*, p39.

Chapter 3: Terrorism

1 Leonard Cole, *The Eleventh Plague*, W H Freeman, 1997, p2.

2 US Senate Permanent Subcommittee on Investigations (Minority Staff), *Global Proliferation of Weapons of Mass Destruction, a Case Study on the Aum Shinrikyo: Hearing Before the Permanent Subcommittee on Investigations*, 104th Congress, 1st Sess., 31 October 1995, p44.

3 Paul Mann, "Mass Weapons Threat Deepens Worldwide", *Aviation Week and Space Technology*, 17 June, 1996, p61.

4 *Ibid*, p59.

5 Thomas W. Frazier and Drew C. Richardson, eds. *Food and Agricultural Security*. Annals of the New York Academy of Sciences, vol 894, 1999.

6 The examples quoted here have been brought together in "Chemical and Biological Terrorism: New threat to public safety?" by Ron Purver, *Conflict Studies* 295, Research Institute for the Study of Conflict and Terrorism, December 1996/January 1997.

7 Staff Statement, US Senate Permanent Subcommittee on Investigations (Minority Staff), Hearings on Global Proliferation of Weapons of Mass Destruction: Response to Domestic Terrorism, 27 March 1996.

8 Robert Taylor, "All fall down", *New Scientist*, 11 May, 1996, pp32–37.

9 Jonathan B. Tucker, "Dilemmas of a Dual-Use Technology: Toxins in Medicine and Warfare", *Politics and the Life Sciences*, Vol 13, No 1, February 1994, pp51–62.

10 Joseph D. Douglass, Jr., and Neil C. Livingstone, *America the Vulnerable: The Threat of Chemical and Biological Warfare*. Lexington Books, Lexington MA, 1987, p23.

11 Quoted in Leonard Cole, *op. cit.*, p4.

12 Mayer, "The Biological Weapon: A Poor Man's Weapon of Mass Destruction", in *Battlefield of the Future*, Air University, 1996.

13 B. Erlick, *Hearings before the Committee on Governmental Affairs and its Permanent Subcommittee on Investigations on Global Spread of Chemical and Biological Weapons*, 101st Congress, 10 February 1989, pp237–41.

14 Personal communication, 4/2/97.

15 Interview with Graham Pearson, 5/7/96.

16 Personal communication, 7 November 1996

17 Staff Statement, *op. cit.*, 27 March 1996.

18 Anti-Terrorism and Effective Death Penalty Act, Pub L No.104–132, signed into law on 24 April 1996.

19 *Federal Register*, Rules and Regulations, Vol 61, No 207, October 24, 1996, p 55196.

20 Michael Moodie, personal communication, 22 January 1997.

21 Personal communication from the Home Office, 31 January 1997

22 Department of Trade and Industry, Strategic Export Controls, The Stationery Office, Cm 3989, July 1998. Also available at http://www.dti.gov.uk/export.control/stratex/

23 "Killer germs on sale for just £600", *Sunday Times*, 22 November 1998, pp1 and 8.

Chapter 4: Iraq's Secret Biological Weapons

1 "Tornados attack aircraft 'built to spray anthrax' ", *The Guardian*, 19 December 1998.

2 UN Security Council Resolution 687 of 3 April, 1991

3 This interview with Rod Barton is edited from *Pacific Research*, May 1996, Vol 9 No 2, pp31–35.

4 Milton Leitenberg, "Biological Weapons and Arms Control", *Contemporary Security Policy*, April 1996, Vol 17 No 1, pp1–79.

5 UN Security Council document S/1995/864, 11 October 1995, para 24.

6 "News Chronology August through November 1995", *Chemical Weapons Convention Bulletin*, No 30, December 1995, p17.

7 Montgomery (Alabama) Advertiser, 24 November 1994, Sec B.

8 Gunilla Floden, Elizabeth French. Peter Jones, Natalie Pauwels and John Pascal Zanders, "Iraq: the UNSCOM Experience", 12 October 1988, at http://www.sipri.se/projects/chembio.html

9 UN Security Council, *op, cit.*, para 28.

10 Paul Rogers, "Extent and Implications of the Iraqi Biological Weapons programme: A Preliminary Note" (unpublished), 21 November 1995.

11 Raymond Zilinskas, "UNSCOM and the UNSCOM experience in Iraq", *Politics and the Life Sciences*, Vol 14, No 2, August 1995, pp230–235.

12 "Chemical and Biological Weapons", POST note 111, Parliamentary Office of Science and Technology, February 1998, p2.

13 "UEA graduate heads Iraqi germs project", *East Anglian Daily Times*, 1 February, 1995.

14 "Gulf cover-up", *Chemistry in Britain*, vol 33 no 12, Dec 1997, p8.

Chapter 5: Brothers in Arms

1 G B Carter, "Biological Warfare and Biological Defence in the United Kingdom 1940–1979", *RUSI Journal*, December 1992, p 67. In fact, the Germans did not develop a BW capability during the War (but see box for their experiments with the Colorado beetle). According to the UK's foremost expert on BW, Julian Perry Robinson, "Hitler is supposed to have suppressed what initiatives there were to develop biological weapons until 1943 when, after German reverses in the USSR, a BW research station was established at Posen under the auspices of the SS . . . the Station . . . was finally evacuated in the face of the Red Army in 1945 without having accomplished anything very startling." See *The Problem of Chemical and Biological Warfare, Vol 1*, Stockholm International Peace Research Institute (SIPRI), Stockholm, 1971, p117.

2 Public Records Office (PRO), Cabinet Papers (CAB) 53/4.

3 John Bryden, *Deadly Allies*, McClelland and Stewart Inc, Toronto, 1989, pp103–4.

4 Carter, *op. cit.*, p67.

5 *Ibid*, p30.

6 Graham Pearson in Preface to G B Carter, *Porton Down: 75 Years of Chemical and Biological Research*, HMSO, London, 1992.

7 A Landsborough Thomson: *Half a Century of Medical Research, Vol 2*, Medical Research Council, London, 1987, pp256–7.

8 Bryden, *op. cit.*, p38.

9 *Ibid*, p50.

10 *Ibid*, p82.

11 Carter, *op. cit.*, p49.

12 Obituary in *The Times*, 12 October, 1971.

13 See box for a description of the Germans' experiments with Colorado beetles—notorious potato pests. Hankey's memorandum cites the discovery of a few between Weymouth and Swansea, on the south coast of England, earlier during 1941; and the implication is that the Germans may have tried to use them against the British potato crop. This in spite of the fact that Hankey admits that

"these are not important potato districts and no containers or other suspicious objects were discovered." PRO, CAB 120/782.

14 Carter, *Porton Down, op. cit.*, p54.

15 UN General Assembly (XXIV), Document A/C.1/PV.1716:102, 9 December 1969.

16 Carter, "Biological Warfare and Biological Defence." *op. cit.*, p70.

17 *FOA informerar om Biological Weapons*, National Defence Research Establishment, Umea, 1995, p25.

18 David Martin, "The Use of Poison and Biological Weapons in the Rhodesian War", Lecture given at University of Zimbabwe, 7 July 1993.

19 Bryden, *op. cit.*, p93.

20 1944 saw a discussion between American military personnel and the administration about whether to destroy Japan's rice crop with the chemical ammonium thiocyanate. The plan was rejected on moral and tactical grounds. See B Bernsteirn, "Origins of the Biological Warfare Program", in Susan Wright (ed), *Preventing a Biological Arms Race*, MIT Press, Cambridge, Mass, 1990, pp18–20.

21 PRO, DEFE 2/1251, minute by Brigadier Wansborough-Jones of 3 December, 1945.

22 Newsnight, 1 May 1981.

23 PRO, PREM 3/89.

24 PRO CAB 79/77, 8 July 1944.

25 PRO PREM 3/89.

26 Robert Kupperman and David Smith, "Coping with Biological Terrorism", in *Biological Weapons: Weapons of the Future?*, ed. Brad Roberts, Significant Issues Series, Vol XV, No 1, Center for Strategic and International Studies, Washington DC, 1993, p38.

27 Malcolm Dando, *Biological Warfare in the 21st Century*, Brassey's, London, 1994, p50.

28 Carter, "Biological Warfare and Biological Defence . . . ", *op. cit.*, p 71

29 *Ibid*, p71.

30 R Harris and J Paxman, *A Higher Form of Killing*, p155.

31 Carter, "Biological Warfare . . . ", *op. cit.*, p71.

32 Bryden, *op. cit.*, p298. Bryden's informant was Dr O M Solandt, who headed Canada's Defence Research Board after the War.

33 Harris and Paxman (*op. cit.*, p158) relate how, from 1957–9, Porton scientists experimented to see how bacteria would spread over the UK in a BW attack. They released harmless chemicals into the atmosphere from planes and monitored their dispersion. They conclude that "Britain was virtually defenceless against a clandestine germ attack."

34 PRO, DEFE 4–3, 26 March 1947.

35 Carter, "Biological Warfare . . . ", *op. cit.*, p71.

36 Bryden, *op. cit.*, p240.

37 Statement to the Conference of the Committee on Disarmament, CCD/PV.460, 24 March 1970.

38 Bryden, *op. cit.*, p242.

39 Susan Wright, "Evolution of Biological Warfare Policy: 1945–1990", in Wright *op. cit.*, p28.

40 *Ibid*, p33.
41 Seymour Hersch, *Chemical and Biological Warfare: America's Hidden Arsenal*, MacGibbon and Kee, London, 1968.
42 George W Christopher, Theodore J Cieslak, Julie A Pavlin, Edward Eitsen Jr, "Biological Warfare: A Historical Perspective", in *Journal of the American Medical Association*, August 6, 1997, Vol 278, No 5, pp412–417.
43 *The Problem of Chemical and Biological Weapons, Vol II*, SIPRI, p122.
44 Christopher et al, *op. cit.*, p414.
45 Robert Harris and Jeremy Paxman, *A Higher Form of Killing*, Chatto and Windus, 1982, p156.
46 Leonard Cole, *Clouds of Secrecy: The Army's Germ Warfare Tests Over Populated Areas*, Savage, MD: Rowman and Littlefield, 1990, pp44–58.
47 Leonard Cole, *The Eleventh Plague*, W H Freeman, 1997.
48 United States Army Chemical Corps, *Summary of Major Events and Problems*, US Army Chemical Corps Historical Office, Army Chemical Center, MD, 1959, pp 107–108.
49 Wright, *op. cit.*, p51
50 John Bryden, *op.cit.*, p120 and footnote 30, p281. The comments were made by Dr Murray Sutton, who had been involved in experiments at the Canadians' testing ground at Suffield, and at Professor G B Reed's laboratory at Queen's University: " . . . I think they [the British on Gruinard] lost some personnel too. Those are the things you will never know because they have people dying of pneumonia—it says 'cause of death pneumonia' or something like that. You will never be able to prove it one way or another."
51 R J Manchee and W D P Stewart: "The Decontamination of Gruinard Island", *Chemistry in Britain*, July 1988, pp690–691.
52 Brian Balmer, "The day germ warfare came to Tooting Broadway", *The Independent*, 28 March 1995.
53 *New Scientist*, 20/27 December, 1984, p8.
54 David Huxsoll et al., "Medicine in Defense Against Biological Warfare", *Journal of the American Medical Association*, Vol 262, No 5, 4 August 1989, p678.
55 A Landsborough Thomson, *Half a Century of Medical Research. Vol 2: The Programme of the Medical Research Council (UK)*. MRC, London, 1987, pp260–1. Poem quoted in G B Carter, *Porton Down*, HMSO, 1992, p41.
56 Landsborough Thomson, *op. cit., p 261*. Sir Edward Mellanby, "Medical Research in Wartime", *British Medical Journal*, 18 September, 1943, p4315.
57 SIPRI, *The problem of Chemical and Biological Warfare, Vol 1*, 1971, p110.
58 Robert Harris and Jeremy Paxman, *A Higher Form of Killing*, Chatto and Windus, 1982.
59 *Ibid*, p93.
60 Erhard Geissler, "More about the Heydrich Assassination", *ASA Newsletter*, 5 December 1996, p10.
61 Julian Perry Robinson, "Environmental effects of chemical and biological warfare" in *War and Environment*, (ed) Wendy Barnaby, Environment Advisory Council, Stockholm, 1981, pp99–100.
62 Lecture by David Martin, Director of the Southern African Research and Documentation Centre in Harare, in the University of Zimbabwe War and Strategic Studies Seminar Series, 7 July 1993.

Chapter 6: Germany, USSR, Japan and South Africa

1 Erhard Geissler, "The German Perspective on the Colorado Beetle During World War II", *ASA Review* 96–6, pp12–16.

2 Erhard Geissler, John Ellis van Courtland Moon and Graham Pearson, "Perceptions and misperceptions, the motives for BTW activities: What can we learn from history?", in Erhard Geissler and John Ellis van Courtland Moon (eds), *Biological and Toxin Weapons Research, Development and Use from the Middle Ages to 1945: A Critical Comparative Analysis*, SIPRI, Oxford University Press 1999.

3 *Ibid*

4 *The Problem of Chemical and Biological Warfare*, Volume 1, SIPRI, 1971, p116.

5 UK Public Record Office, file CAB 120/782.

6 *Ibid*

7 Geissler, van Courtland Moon and Pearson, *op. cit.*

8 Geissler, *APA Review, op. cit.* p14.

9 *Ibid*, p15.

10 Benjamin C. Garrett, "The Colorado Potato Beetle Goes to War", *Chemical Weapons Convention Bulletin*, Issue No. 33, September 1996, pp2–3.

11 Geissler, *ASA Review, op. cit.*, p15.

12 *Ibid.*

13 See Geissler and van Courtland Moon (eds)., *op. cit.*

14 Stockholm International Peace Research Institute, *The Problem of Chemical and Biological Warfare*, Vol 1: "The Rise of CB Weapons", Almqvist & Wiksell, Stockholm, 1971, p222

15 Robert Harris and Jeremy Paxman, *A Higher Form of Killing*, Chatto & Windus, 1982, p142.

16 See Leonard Cole, "Sverdlovsk, Yellow Rain, and Novel Soviet Bioweapons: Allegations and Responses", in *Preventing a Biological Arms Race*, ed Susan Wright, MIT Press, Massachusetts, 1990, p200.

17 SIPRI (Stockholm International Peace Research Institute) Yearbook, 1993, Oxford University Press, 1993, p288.

18 Quoted in SIPRI (Stockholm International Peace Research Institute) Yearbook 1994, Oxford University Press, 1994, pp716–7. For a more detailed account of the Russian military microbiological effort, see "From Military to Industrial Complex? The Conversion of Military Microbiological Facilities in the Russian Federation" by Anthony Rimmington, in *Contemporary Security Policy*, Vol 17, No 1, April 1996, pp80–112.

19 Anthony Rimmington, *op. cit.*, p.88.

20 Quoted in Robert Harris and Jeremy Paxman, *A Higher Form of Killing*, Chatto and Windus, 1982, p79.

21 Before and during the War, the British carried out tests of chemical weapons at Porton. After 1941, they tested mustard gas on British soldiers at Porton Down, and on Canadians, Australians and Indians in their own countries. John Bryden in *Deadly Allies* (McClelland and Stewart, Toronto, 1989, pp168–175), gives details of some of these trials. Canadian soldiers were exposed to mustard gas at Suffield, the Canadians' huge testing ground in Alberta. Australian soldiers at Innisfail in Queensland were also exposed to various agents in a steel chamber. The US officer observing these tests reported back to his superiors: "It is impor-

tant to keep in mind the keen individual pride in physical prowess inbred in each Australian when comparing casualties obtained here and in other countries. The men who are classed as casualties here, are truly casualties." (*ibid*, p.172.) The most horrific tests seem to have been those carried out on "British" (Indian personnel) troops in Karachi, now in Pakistan, in 1943. Bryden writes that dozens of men "were paraded around in the mid-day heat on mustard-soaked ground . . . The men wore various degrees of protection and from their injuries it was deduced that a man's scrotum appeared to be particularly vulnerable to mustard effects . . . Five men were then selected to receive especially long exposures with no protection whatsoever. The results were horrific . . . The injuries to the genital areas of the five men were grotesque and they suffered 'intense and crippling pain' . . . After a month two were diagnosed as having developed 'a slightly morbid genital consciousness'."—*Ibid*, p173.

22 British Intelligence Objectives Sub-Committee Report on Scientific Intelligence Survey in Japan, Vol V: Biological Warfare (September and October 1945); quoted in Robert Harris and Jeremy Paxman, *A higher Form of Killing*, Chatto and Windus, London 1982, p78.

23 The following descriptions are taken from *Factories of Death* by Sheldon Harris, Routledge, 1994.

24 Harris, *Ibid*, p27.

25 *Ibid*, p28.

26 Quoted in *Ibid*, p70.

27 Harris, *Ibid*, p67.

28 Peter Williams and David Wallace, *Unit 731*, Hodder and Stoughton, London, 1898

29 *Ibid*, p59.

30 See Harris, *op. cit.*, p130.

31 Edwin V. Hill to General Alden C. Waitt, Chief, Chemical Corps, 12 December, 1947, The National Archives; quoted in Harris, *op. cit.*, pp191, 207.

32 *Ibid*, p221.

33 Wallace and Williams, *op. cit.*, p286.

34 Richard Burt, quoted in Leonard Cole, *op.cit.*, p203.

35 Quoted in "Yellow Rain in Southeast Asia: The Story Collapses" by Julian Perry Robinson, Jeanne Guillemin and Matthew Meselson, in *Preventing a Biological Arms Race*, edited by Susan Wright, MIT Press, Massachusetts, 1990, p222.

36 *Ibid*, p225.

37 Thomas D. Seeley, Joan W. Nowicke, Matthew Meselson, Jeanne Guillemin, Pongthep Akratanakul, "Yellow Rain", *Scientific American* 253, No.3 (September 1985), pp128–37.

38 Quoted in Perry Robinson, Guillemin and Meselson, *op. cit.*, p234.

39 Quoted in "Microbes in the Service of the State" by Sarah Leibovitz-Dar, Hadashot Supplement, 13.8.1993.

40 *Ibid*

41 *Ibid*

42 See "Klingberg was to be part of 3–way spy swap", *The Jerusalem Post*, 6 August 1993.

43 P.R. Kumaraswamy, "Marcus Klingberg and Israel's 'biological option' ", *Middle East International*, 16 August 1996, pp21–22.

Chapter 7: Scientific Developments and BW

1 John E. Smith, *Biotechnology*, Third Edition, Cambridge University Press, 1996, p2.
2 *Ibid*, p49.
3 Jonathan Tucker, "The Future of Biological Warfare", in *The Proliferation of Advanced Weaponry*, edited by W. Thomas Wander and Eric Arnett, American Association for the Advancement of Science, 1992, p61.
4 *Ibid*, p61.
5 John E. Smith, *op. cit.*, p38.
6 SIPRI Yearbook 1993, p294.
7 Jeffrey Almond, "Understanding the Molecular Basis of Infectious Disease: Implications for Biological Weapons Development", *Bailrigg*, Memorandum 16, Centre for Strategic Studies, University of Lancaster, 1996.
8 T Horimoto and Y Kawaoka, "Reverse genetics provides direct evidence for a correlation of hemagglutinin cleavability and virulence of an avian influenza A virus", *J. Virol.* 68, 1994, pp3120–3128.
9 Jeffrey Almond, personal communication, 8 November, 1996.
10 Jeffrey Almond, *op. cit.*, p41.
11 Richard Novick and Seth Shulman, "New Forms of Biological Warfare?", in *Preventing a Biological Arms Race*, edited by Susan Wright, MIT Press, Cambridge, Mass, 1990, p113.
12 Rachel Nowak, "Bacterial Genome Sequence Bagged", *Science*, V.268, 28 July 1995, pp468–470.)
13 SIPRI Yearbook 1993, p303.
14 "Genetic weapons: Could the latest research add a terrifying new dimension to warfare?" *Foreign Report*, Jane's Information Group, 14 March, 1996.
15 Quoted in an interview with Cohen in *Jane's Defence Weekly*, 13 August 1997.
16 Shriver MD et al, "Ethnic affiliation by use of population-specific DNA markers", *American Journal of Human Genetics*, 60, 1997, 957–64.
17 See, for example, Susan Aldridge, *The Thread of Life: the story of genes and genetic engineering*, Cambridge University Press (Canto Imprint), 1998, pp173–79.
18 Cary Fowler and Pat Mooney, *The Threatened Gene*, Lutterworth Press, 1990.
19 Malcolm Dando, *Biological Warfare in the 21st Century*, Brassey's, 1994, p156.
20 Lt Col Terry N. Mayer, "The Biological Weapon: A Poor Nation's Weapon of Mass Destruction", in *Battlefield of the Future*, Air University, 1995.

Chapter 8: Defense against Biological Warfare

1 Published by W H Freeman, New York, 1997.
2 Uriel Elchalal *et al.*, "Delivery with gas mask during missile attack", *The Lancet*, Vol 337, January 26, 1991, p242.
3 *Dealing with Disaster*, HMSO, 1992.
4 Graham Pearson, "Chemical and Biological Defence: An Essential National Security Requirement", in *RUSI Journal*, Vol 140, No 4, August 1995, p24.
5 "File on Four", BBC Radio 4, 22? January 1997.
6 Personal communication, 21 January 1997.
7 Karl Lowe, Graham Pearson, Victor Utgoff, "Potential Values of a Simple BW Protective Mask", IDA Paper P-3077, September 1995.

8 NATO Handbook on Medical Aspects of NBC Defensive Operations, Part II Biological, October 1992.

9 Clifford Beal, "An Invisible Enemy", *International Defense Review* 3, 1995, pp36–41.

10 "Newest DARPA Initiatives Focus on MEMS Dust, Anti-Biowarfare", Defense Week, Vol.17, Issue 15, 8 April 1996.

11 CBDE Annual Report and Accounts, 1994/95, London, HMSO, p14.

12 "Quick test on viruses developed", Roger Highfield, *Daily Telegraph,* 22 July 1995, p7.

13 Clifford Beal, *op. cit.,* p41.

14 Erhard Geissler, John Ellis van Courtland Moon and Graham Pearson, "Perceptions and misperceptions, the motives for BTW activities: What can we learn from history?", in *Biological and Toxin Weapons Research, Development and Use from the Middle Ages to 1945: A Critical Comparative Analysis,* Erhard Geissler and John Ellis van Courtland Moon (eds), SIPRI, Oxford University Press, forthcoming.

15 *Brief History of the Kwantong Army Anti-Epidemic Water Supply Unit,* submitted to a Diet Committee from the Japanese Ministry of Health and Welfare in 1982. Quoted in K. Tsuneishi, *Target: Ishii Japanese Biological Warfare Activity and Investigation on it by US,* Nagasaki, 1985.

16 Statement by the US representative at the Fourth Review Conference of the Biological Weapons Convention, November 1996.

17 J. King and H. Strauss, *op.cit.,* p131.

18 *Ibid,* p122

19 *Ibid,* p125.

20 Paul Mann, "Detection Sensors Crucial, but Technically Exacting", *Aviation Week and Space Technology,* 17 June, 1996, pp66–69.

21 Geissler and van Courtland Moon (eds), *op. cit.,* describe how faulty intelligence and the suspicions it aroused fuelled these early BW programmes: "The BTW programmes of the major belligerents were fuelled largely by their respective intelligence perceptions at the time. Although enemy activities in BTW preparedness were extremely difficult to identify accurately, there was a widespread appreciation that everyone else was preparing for BTW. The difficulties in determining whether the programmes were merely defensive meant that suspicions regarding enemy intentions fuelled the arms effort."

22 D Huxsoll et al, "Medicine in Defense Against Biological Warfare", *Journal of the American Medical Association,* 4 August 1989, vol 262, No 5, pp677–679.

23 Leonard Cole, *The Eleventh Plague,* W H Freeman, 1997, pp 65–66. Cole argues that inactivated plague bacteria could become re-activated under certain circumstances.

24 D Huxsoll et al, *op. cit.,* p679.

25 C Piller and K Yamamoto, "The US Biological Defense Research Program in the 1980s", in *Preventing a Biological Arms Race, op. cit.,* p136.

26 US Senate Sub-committee on Oversight of Government Management of the Committee of Governmental Affairs, *Department of Defense Safety Programs for Chemical and Biological Warfare Research: Hearings before the Subcommittee on Oversight of Government Management,* 100th Congress, 2nd sess., 27–8 July, 1988, 3.

27 US Department of the Army, US Medical Research and Development Command, Final Programmatic Environmental Impact Statement, "Biological Defense Research Program", Fort Detrick, Frederick, MD, April 1989, ES-6.
28 Leonard Cole, *op. cit.*, Chapter 3.
29 *The Independent*, 9 May, 1990.
30 Malcolm Dando, *Biological Warfare in the 21st Century*, Brassey's, 1994, p 190.
31 *Hansard*, 16 January 1996, p530.
32 Quoted in Sally Lehrman, "Major waste reported in biowarfare defense", *San Francisco Examiner*, 28 January 1991, p A-8.

Chapter 9: International Regulation

1 Statement by US representative to the Fourth Review Conference of the BWC, Geneva, November 1996.
2 Alexander V. Vorobiev, "Working on the Compliance Regime for the BWC", *Chemical Weapons Convention Bulletin:* Quarterly Journal of the Harvard Sussex Program on CBW Armament and Arms Limitation, Issue No. 31, March 1966, p2.
3 Some of these programmes have been set up as a result of *Agenda 21* that followed the Rio Summit of 1992; others come under the 1992 Convention on Biological Diversity. See "Implementing Article X of the BTWC: Avoiding Duplication", by Graham Pearson, *Chemical Weapons Convention Bulletin*, Issue No. 32, June 1996. There is a debate about the scope of bilateral and multilateral activity that can be said to be relevant to Article X of the BWC: see Erhard Geissler, Iris Hunger and Ernst Bruder, "Implementing Article X of the Biological Weapons Convention", in Oliver Thranert (ed), *Enhancing the Biological Weapons Convention*, Verlag J.H.W. Dietz Nachfolger, 1996
4 Julian Perry Robinson, "Some Political Aspects of the Control of Biological Weapons", *Science in Parliament*, Vol 53 No 3, May/June 1996, p11.
5 *Scientific Aspects of Control of Biological Weapons*, The Royal Society, 1995, p48.
6 Malcolm Dando, *Biological Warfare in the 21st Century*, Brassey's, 1994, p193–4.
7 R C Imrie, "An Industry View of Verification", Paper presented at NATO Advanced Workshop, Budapest, March 28–30 1996.
8 *Ibid*, p4.
9 See J R Walker (Arms Control and Disarmament Research Unit, Foreign and Commonwealth Office),and A P Phillips and L Miller (both from CBDE Porton Down), "Up-Date: Verification of the Biological and Toxin Weapons Convention and the UK's Practice Compliance Inspection Programme", *Verification '96*, John Poole and Richard Guthrie (eds), Verification Technology Information Centre, Westview Press, Oxford.
10 University of Bradford BWTC Project Briefing Paper No. 17: "The Strengthened BTWC Protocol: Implications for the Biotechnology and Pharmaceutical Industry." October 1998.
11 "Criminalizing BW", *Chemical Weapons Convention Bulletin*, Issue No.31, March 1996.

12 "Programme for countering emerging infectious diseases (ProCEID) by prophylactic, diagnostic and therapeutic measures", Meeting Report, *Biologicals*,
24, 71–4, 1996.
13 Graham Pearson, personal communication, 5 July 1996.

Chapter 10: By Opposing End Them

1 M.Lappe, "Ethics in Biological Warfare Research", in Susan Wright (ed), *Preventing a Biological Arms Race*, MIT Press, 1990.
2 *Ibid*, p93.
3 Sir Joseph Rotblat, personal communication, 24 January, 1997.
4 Robert L. Sinsheimer, "Scientists and Research", in Susan Wright, *op. cit.*
5 Graham S. Pearson and Malcolm Dando (eds), *Strengthening the Biological
Weapons Convention: Key Points for the Fourth Review Conference* (Geneva: QUNO,
1996).
6 Association for Clinical Research in the Pharmaceutical Industry, Biochemical
Society, British Crop Protection Council, British Society for Immunology,
British Society for Plant Pathology, British Toxicology Society, Genetical Society, Institute of Biology, Society for Applied Bacteriology and Society for General Microbiology.
7 "Scientific Aspects of Control of Biological Weapons", The Royal Society, 1994.
8 John Bulloch and Harvey Morris, *The Gulf War: Its Origins, History and Consequences*, Methuen, London, 1989, p259.
9 Flora Lewis, "Move to Stop Iraq", *New York Times*, 14 September 1988, Sec A-31.
10 US Senate Committee on Foreign Relations, *Chemical and Biological Weapons
Threat—The Urgent Need for Remedies: Hearings Before the Committee on Foreign
Relations*, 101st Congress, 1st sess., 24 January, 1 March and 9 May, 1989, p30.
11 Interview with Sue Mayer, 17 July, 1996.

INDEX